m Classics

Film Classics is a series of bo.... that introduces, interprets
**Martial** :brates landmarks of world cinema. Each volume offers an
**Tel: 019** 'nt for the film's 'classic' status, together with discussion of its
‾ion and reception history, its place within a genre or national
, an account of its technical and aesthetic importance and, in
1ses, the author's personal response to the film.

ll list of titles available in the series, please visit our website:
lgrave.com/bfi

ently concentrated examples of flowing freeform critical poetry.'

able body of work collectively generating some fascinating insights
volution of cinema.'
*her Education Supplement*

:s is a landmark in film criticism.'
*ly Review of Film and Video*

v the most bountiful book series in the history of film criticism.'
n Rosenbaum, *Film Comment*

# From Here to Eternity

J. E. Smyth

A BFI book published by Palgrave

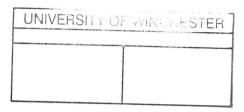
© J. E. Smyth 2015

First published in 2015 by
**PALGRAVE**

on behalf of the

**BRITISH FILM INSTITUTE**
21 Stephen Street, London W1T 1LN
www.bfi.org.uk

There's more to discover about film and television through the BFI. Our world-renowned archive, cinemas, festivals, films, publications and learning resources are here to inspire you.

Palgrave in the UK is an imprint of Macmillan Publishers Limited, registered in England, company number 785998, of 4 Crinan Street, London N1 9XW. Palgrave Macmillan in the US is a division of St Martin's Press LLC, 175 Fifth Avenue, New York, NY 10010. Palgrave is a global imprint of the above companies and is represented throughout the world. Palgrave® and Macmillan® are registered trademarks in the United States, the United Kingdom, Europe and other countries.

Front cover design: Eda Akaltun
Series text design: ketchup/SE14
Images from *From Here to Eternity* (Fred Zinnemann, 1953), © Columbia Pictures Corporation; *Julia* (Fred Zinnemann, 1977), Twentieth Century-Fox Film Corporation

Set by Cambrian Typesetters, Camberley, Surrey
Printed in China

This book is printed on paper suitable for recycling and made from fully managed and sustained forest sources. Logging, pulping and manufacturing processes are expected to conform to the environmental regulations of the country of origin.

British Library Cataloguing-in-Publication Data
A catalogue record for this book is available from the British Library
A catalog record for this book is available from the Library of Congress

ISBN 978–1–84457–814–6

# Contents

## Acknowledgments

My thanks to Ned Comstock, Jenny Romero and Barbara Hall for locating archival material, and to Jenna Steventon, Lucinda Knight, Chantal Latchford and Sophia Contento for expert editing and support. My continuing gratitude to Tim Zinnemann for his tolerance and dry humour, and to Alvin Sargent and Stanley for being there. My love to Zoe and Zachary, who side with Maggio every time, and who already know the freedoms and frustrations of exile.

# 'From Here to Eternity'

*'Something like "Eternity" happens only once in a long, long time.'*[1]

Buddy Adler, 1954

It took James Jones 858 pages to tell *From Here to Eternity*'s story of the US army in the last months before the Japanese attack on Pearl Harbor, but the film is as lean and powerful as its star Burt Lancaster's body. Columbia Pictures studio head Harry Cohn wanted the adaptation of the cumbersome bestselling novel to run under two hours, and it does so with almost military precision. From the first shot, soldiers move into line, forming their companies while George Duning's musical score covers the opening titles. These are men who fit into the spaces of their platoons and companies as neatly as any wartime combat film fit the Hollywood studio production line. But though any individuality or differences among the men disappear as they begin to drill in the neat courtyards of Schofield Barracks, Hollywood had never produced a film like *From Here to Eternity*. It was and is a standalone original, much like its two protagonists, First Sergeant Milton Warden (Burt Lancaster) and Private Robert E. Lee Prewitt (Montgomery Clift).

The film charts the lives of five lonely and disillusioned people living in the last prewar days of Pearl Harbor under the shadow of America's pacific military empire. Private Robert E. Lee Prewitt has just transferred from the Bugle Corps to the infantry at Schofield Barracks, Oahu, Hawaii. Stubborn, principled, loyal and a disciplined and capable soldier, he's doomed in the nepotistic peacetime US army. His new 'topkick', Sergeant Milton Warden, is initially wary and disapproving of the outsider, but grows to like him, even as company commander Captain Dana Holmes (Philip Ober) pushes Prewitt to the edge with a brutal and unrelenting hazing campaign designed to force him to box on the regimental team. Warden, disgusted with his superior officer and bored with army routine, has an affair with Holmes's wife Karen (Deborah Kerr). Trapped in a loveless marriage and known up and down the base for her string of affairs with enlisted men, she ends up falling in love with Warden. Meanwhile, Prewitt takes up with a prostitute called Lorene (Donna Reed) who works at the New Congress Club in downtown Honolulu. His friend Angelo Maggio (Frank Sinatra) is even more outspoken than Prewitt and ends up being sent to the stockade where he is beaten to the point of death by Sergeant Judson (Ernest Borgnine). Prewitt later kills Judson outside the New Congress Club and goes AWOL, but tries to return to his unit shortly after the Japanese bomb Pearl Harbor. He's shot by his own men. A few days later, Karen and Lorene sail for the states, but Warden remains at Pearl Harbor, poised for a heroic war career.

Part war picture, part romantic melodrama, part historical period piece, part social realist film, *From Here to Eternity* fit into no neat genre. Made at the end of the studio system in the chaotic media age of television, 3D, CinemaScope, and stereophonic sound, it nonetheless was shot in spare black-and-white and in the standard aspect ratio and, as critic Archer Winsten first argued, 'does not need' the 'enhancements' of new cinematic technology.[2] It became one of the biggest box-office hits of the decade, pulling in $30 million in rentals ($270 million in today's currency).[3] Adapted by a small-time screenwriter, a foreign-born, art-house director, and a little-known producer, *From Here to Eternity* would go on to define the careers of Daniel Taradash, Fred Zinnemann and Buddy Adler, earning thirteen Academy Award nominations and winning eight Oscars, a feat only equalled by *Gone with the Wind* (1939). Often characterised as a star-studded production, the film featured a washed-up radio heartthrob, a British-born 'lady' imported from MGM and a New York method actor who made his name as an unrepentant outsider and a barely concealed bisexual. Even today, the film careers of Frank Sinatra, Deborah Kerr and Montgomery Clift are defined in great

part by their roles in *From Here to Eternity*. At the time of its release in August 1953, the only obvious star in the cast was Burt Lancaster (*The Killers*, 1946; *Brute Force*, 1947; *Criss Cross*, 1949; *Jim Thorpe, All-American*, 1950). Lancaster and Kerr's horizontal kiss in the surf at Halona Cove Beach worried Hollywood censors at the Production Code Administration (PCA), and was the focus of several racy photographic spreads in *Picturegoer* and *Look* before it went on to become 'one of the classic moments in film history',[4] but it was a relatively minor issue for the US government and armed forces. More troublesome was *From Here to Eternity*'s portrait of the US army, which pulled no punches in its revelations of nepotism, bureaucratic corruption, sadism, fascism, prostitution, class prejudice, adultery and homosexuality. The film was also made at the height of Hollywood's anticommunist 'red scare' by film-makers who had already felt the political heat for their nonconformist views. As Zinnemann recalled, 'McCarthyism was still very much alive, and filming a book so openly scathing about the peacetime army ... was regarded by many as foolhardy if not downright subversive'.[5]

Though contemporary audiences and critics praised the film's controversial narrative and professional style, more recent appraisals by a number of historians and critics have tended to view the film as both a popular endorsement of hegemonic masculinity and a classic example of 1950s Hollywood compromise, in which Jones's profane original text was censored by the PCA and the US military establishment.[6] As Steven J. Whitfield has commented: 'If it had been critical of the military, a movie version would have been not only intolerable, but, in the 1950s, also inconceivable'. But these appraisals of *From Here to Eternity*'s 'conformism' are based on very marginal knowledge of the film's production history. In this book at least, *From Here to Eternity*'s film-makers call the interpretive shots. Fred Zinnemann's extensive collection of script, research and editing notes, Daniel Taradash's many draft scripts and oral history, Buddy Adler's production memos, Columbia Pictures publicity, PCA complaints and military correspondence are all used to reconstruct just how uniquely controversial the film was, not only in terms of its portrait of a corrupt military, but also in terms of its revelations about racism, sexuality, adultery, political exploitation and the unresolved legacy of World War II. Rather than promoting Cold War images of the unassailable American male, *From Here to Eternity*'s film-makers looked back at a more complicated prewar era and kept working-class nobodies, ethnic minorities and women in the frame, articulating a voice of anti-consensus on the margins of American empire.

\*   \*   \*

Although the Hollywood studios relied on adapting bestselling novels to attract big box office, most critics and industry insiders believed that *From Here to Eternity* was 'unfilmable', despite being the number one bestseller of 1951.[7] Although the chatter in the New York papers was all about the book's profanity and explicit sex scenes, Bert Bloch at Twentieth Century-Fox turned it down, saying he 'didn't see how it could be a picture', since 'it could be made only with the cooperation of the army'.[8] Harry Cohn, longtime head of Columbia Pictures, knew he could handle the military establishment, and purchased the rights in the spring of 1951 for $82,000.[9] The joke in Hollywood was that the famously rough-talking Cohn had purchased the 'dirty book' because ' "he thinks everybody talks that way" '.[10] But not everybody dared to talk about the US army the way Jones did.

James Jones enlisted in the army in 1939 and served in the 25th Infantry Division (27th Infantry Regiment) stationed at Schofield. Wounded in action, he began to write of his wartime experiences as a kind of post-trauma therapy. After abandoning his first novel, he wrote *From Here to Eternity* and Scribner's, Ernest Hemingway and F. Scott Fitzgerald's publishing house, took the young novelist on. The book shocked most readers in 1951, but celebrity war novelist Norman Mailer (*The Naked and the Dead*, 1948), liked it (although he thought it was an 'awful title'), writing to Jones's editor Burroughs Mitchell, '[I]f the very good is mixed with the sometimes bad, those

Shocking the censors: Buddy Adler reads to a laughing Frank Sinatra and Montgomery Clift, while James Jones looks on (AMPAS)

qualities are inseparable from the author' who 'borrows from no writer I know'.[11]

Jones's contempt for the officer class defined the book; the US army was between wars, and the only action officers saw was in the bedroom with their colleagues' wives. Warden, a model soldier and enlisted man who has risen in the ranks to First Sergeant, manages an army company at Schofield Barracks, Hawaii while his incompetent commander, Captain Dana Holmes, spends his days overseeing the training of non-commissioned officers for the regimental boxing championship and his nights screwing around with a succession of women. 'Warden had a theory about officers: Being an officer would make a son of a bitch out of Christ himself.'[12] The author's sympathy was for some of the thirty-year enlistees, a motley multiethnic and racial crew who boxed to get their commissions, paid for prostitutes when they could afford it and went out with gay men when they couldn't buy their own drinks. The islanders looked down on them as a subclass of white men that had just joined the army to escape the poverty and unemployment of the Great Depression. One of these was Private Robert E. Lee Prewitt, who, at the beginning of the novel, has quit his soft job in the base's Bugle Corps to take a reduction in rank in the infantry. Though named after one of America's iconic 'gentleman' rebels, Prewitt is a poor southerner, the son of a miner killed in a strike.[13] He used to box in his spare time, but quit after one of his punches blinded a friend. When he won't cave in to Captain Holmes's demands to box for the company, Holmes orders one of the most gruelling hazing campaigns in American literature. One of the most likeable protagonists in the novel is sectioned, another is a communist and Prewitt is mistakenly shot by his own men. The staff sergeant of the stockade is a sadist who occasionally beats prisoners to death for fun.

The novel was hardly a good recruitment tool for the Korean War (1950–3), and its cultural impact cast a shadow over the image of the US military wrought by the so-called 'Good War' (1939–45).

'Personal meanness, intrigue, and favoritism can be expected everywhere in life', wrote one *New York Times* critic.

But that the gigantic power of a military organisation should be used in contradiction of its own laws to break one individual standing up for his rights is a travesty of decency. Mr. Jones leaves us no doubt that such a thing could happen. And when he describes the sadistic tortures inflicted in the punishment 'stockade' he leaves his sickened and enraged readers wondering how much American army practices duplicate those of the totalitarian nations.[14]

Fascism, it seemed, was not just a European disease.

Shortly before publication, Mitchell wrote to Jones, 'God knows what Hollywood would do with your book, but you never can tell.'[15] Jones, confident that *From Here to Eternity* would turn him into a literary star just like Norman Mailer, responded that he only wanted two things from Hollywood and the

main one is that I get as much money out of the sale as I can, and to hell with how they butcher it up … I don't give a damn what they do to the movie; the book will stand by itself after the movie is forgotten.[16]

Ironically, the reverse has proved true. In 2011, daughter Kaylie Jones revealed the extent to which Scribner's censored material in Jones's original manuscript which had frankly discussed Private Angelo Maggio getting blowjobs from his wealthy friend, Hal, and other soldiers' sexual relations with men.[17] The book was already 'butchered' by its publishers, and, as things turned out, Jones caved into censorship far more readily than any of *From Here to Eternity*'s film production crew.

As soon as the deal was struck with Columbia, Jones indicated that he wanted to write the script, and Cohn's original producer, Sylvan Simon, hired him. But Jones's treatment was so expurgated and tame (Karen Holmes became the Captain's 'sister' and therefore avoided the issue of marital infidelity and Prewitt was shot by the Japanese rather than by American soldiers), Cohn fired him. Since he bought the property, connections had been warning him

there exists in Washington a feeling against this book because, according to an officer who volunteered information, 'the book portrays a rotten and corrupt army, it propagandises against officers and the tradition of the service, and it could be a demoralising influence at a time when this country's trying to build a big army, draft eighteen-year-olds and win the confidence of parents and Congress'.[18]

But, even worse, the army knew that Jones had portrayed the army as a fascist organisation reminiscent of Hitler's Germany. As Colonel Frank Dorn complained, 'The entire stockade business sounds like a Nazi concentration camp'.[19] It certainly didn't help that at the time, the US was not only purging its own brand of 'outsiders' in Hollywood and the State Department, but also that the US military was planning to collaborate with Spanish leader Francisco Franco's fascist government by trading US oil for Spanish territory to build military bases in Rota, Morón, Zaragosa and Torrejón de Ardoz.

Other executives believed that 'this story must be pro-army' and advised Cohn to 'wave the flag more' if he wanted it to have any chance of being made.[20] But Cohn was adamant. As he explained to Jones,

Have we not changed certain characters in order to pacify the army and thus lost the quality and theme which you tried to put forth in your novel? I feel that the implications in the novel of officer laxity and improper use of authority were so astonishing that it opened the eyes of all who read it. If in making the movie we eliminate this entirely, then we have bastardised the book and cleaned it up to present it for screen purposes without integrity.[21]

Harry Cohn (left) lays a paternal hand on star Burt Lancaster (BFI)

But by then, Sylvan Simon had been dead for over a month, the result of an unexpected heart attack. Cohn replaced him with Buddy Adler. It was one of the smartest decisions Cohn made in his long career.

Though more recent histories of the film's production tend to focus on Taradash and Zinnemann as the picture's principal 'authors', Buddy Adler's role should not be underestimated. Due to his success with *From Here to Eternity*, Adler would quit his job with Cohn to replace the legendary Darryl F. Zanuck as vice-president in charge of production at Twentieth Century-Fox. Like Zanuck, Adler got his start in Hollywood as a writer. The University of Pennsylvania graduate wrote dozens of short subjects for Jack Chertok at MGM in the 1930s (where he would meet the young Fred Zinnemann), and *Quicker Than a Wink* (1940) won Adler his first Academy Award. But Adler had other skills which suited him to *From Here to Eternity*. He was in charge of the Motion Picture Division of the Army Pictorial Service during the war, was decorated with the Legion of Merit for his action in the Philippines with the Signal Corps, and maintained strong connections with the military. At the time of *From Here to Eternity*, he was still a lieutenant colonel in the active reserve. His background and gift of friendly persuasion (they nicknamed him 'Buddy' for a reason), avoided a public-relations breakdown with the military. As he later joked about the production, 'I felt like only half of a civilian'.[22]

In his lengthy oral history with Barbara Hall, Taradash would argue that the film was unscathed by army censorship largely because of Adler. He knew how to get touchy subjects past screen censors; Adler's *No Sad Songs for Me* (1950), 'another Columbia movie that "couldn't be made"', starring Margaret Sullavan, focused on the debilitating effects of cancer. 'I'm not sure anybody but Buddy Adler could have swung the whole thing', said Taradash. 'I think they were very impressed with the fact that Columbia had a former lieutenant colonel in charge of this project, and a very articulate one, too.'[23] But Adler was lucky in getting the Kentucky-born Taradash, who literally appeared out of the blue one morning at story editor Eve Ettinger's

desk in the late summer of 1951 and told her how he would 'lick' the book: Maggio had to die from his beatings in the stockade and Prewitt had to play 'Taps' for him. As Taradash recalled,

The idea of Maggio dying was a large key for me. It was a major step – because in the book, Maggio doesn't die. About halfway through the novel the Army discharges Maggio on a 'Section 8'. That's mental impairment in his case.[24]

The writer also knew where he wanted to end the film: 'with the two women on the ship leaving for Hawaii'.[25] That, he felt, was a more 'logical' ending, though Jones had gone on for an additional hundred-plus pages after the women left the action. Ettinger, intrigued, got Taradash his appointment with Adler, and Adler 'liked every word'.[26] After a surreal story conference in Harry Cohn's gigantic bedroom, they hired Taradash that October. Adler was instrumental in getting Taradash a percentage of the net profits. It was a good deal for a writer but, as Taradash laughed, 'Fred Zinnemann, who came in much later, got two and a half percent for seven years, but that's because *he* had an agent'.[27]

Oscar Night: 25 March 1954 (L–R) Fred Zinnemann, Donna Reed, Buddy Adler and Daniel Taradash (AMPAS)

Cohn was happy. Early in production, executives had worried him about how nasty the army could get if he decided to resist attempts at censoring the content. There was the issue of whether it would withhold archival footage of the Pearl Harbor attacks (considered a requirement given it was the historical grand finale of the film).[28] Luckily, Cohn discovered the military didn't have a copyright on the footage since Fox Movietone cameraman Al Brick had accidentally been out to shoot exteriors for *To the Shores of Tripoli* (1942) on 7 December and caught everything. The footage was later used by cinematographer Gregg Toland for the Academy Award-winning documentary *December 7th* (1943) he co-directed with John Ford, and could be appropriated easily for Columbia's new production. But then there was the question of locations and equipment (uniforms, guns and planes); this film just couldn't be shot on the Columbia lot.

PCA censorship was another potential irritant; in the past, Joseph Breen's office had done whatever it could at script stage to ban rough language and any suggestion of sex. But as Taradash remembered,

The whole business with the Production Code was merely, as I say, to subvert it, to get *around* it. It was not to comply with it, never. As we sat down to do *From Here to Eternity*, I remember Cohn saying, 'We're going to get away with everything we can'. The general attitude was that's how you handle this nonsense.[29]

The more enterprising Hollywood film-makers had a proven strategy for getting what they wanted past the censors, Taradash revealed.

Often you would overdo something so that you could drop back to what you *wanted* to do, because you knew that they'd be very horrified, and if you said, 'Well, suppose we do it this way', which is the way you intended to do it, they'd say, 'That's a pretty good idea, you know?' And if you'd thrown that to them originally, they would have said, 'This is very dangerous stuff here'. That was done all the time, too, playing games with them.[30]

Taradash saw five troublesome aspects of the book the army and censors would want to cut and jotted them down early on: 'The prostitute. The officer's wife. Bloom. Stockade. Queers'.[31] Like Cohn and Adler, he didn't want to sacrifice any of the controversial aspects, and strategised: 'Best approach is to hit hardest and compromise later, if [I] have to, on things kept from the book'.[32] He figured he would have to erase Bloom, the soldier who was hazed for allegedly being gay, and rethink when 'Maggio throws a big scene the night they go to the queers and is sent to the stockade'.[33] But there were certain references to gay relationships in the military he wanted to try and 'slip by' the Production Code, and the military corruption and brutality were essential. By 15 January 1952, Taradash had finished the first treatment which has the bulk of the story as we know it today: Prewitt's abuse at the hands of officers, the twin romances between Warden and Karen and Prewitt and the prostitute Lorene (who was *always* called a prostitute in the script and production notes), Maggio's death and, in a move to 'pre-empt' any attempted army censorship, Holmes's resignation from the army over his treatment of Prewitt.

Adler and Taradash sent a copy off to the army and met with them on 19 February. Some historians have theorised that Adler and Cohn kowtowed to the military and were afraid of being branded or targeted by the establishment: the 1950s are often viewed as an era of compromise and consensus, and so, historians have reasoned, any film produced in that time period must conform to this ideological pattern.[34] Setting these arguments aside, it is true that in order to get the military equipment and agreements to shoot on location in Hawaii, Adler needed to persuade the military liaison that the film would not damage the reputation of the army. For anyone who had read the book, it seemed an impossible task. Taradash recalled that

Cohn had announced ... that he would not do this picture if we couldn't get army cooperation. I didn't accept that, and happily it turned out we didn't have to worry about it, because I felt we could do it without the army helping us.[35]

Although the military was pleasantly surprised that Taradash had eliminated one of their major problems with the book – Captain Holmes's promotion – Colonel Frank Dorn and Colonel Clair Towne had many other objections to the content. Dorn advised Columbia to portray Maggio, the army's mouthiest critic, as 'a parasite on society' because he failed to fit in with the army. Towne, part of the motion-picture section of the Defense Department's Office of Public Information, targeted Maggio, Warden and Prewitt and tried to persuade Adler and Taradash to label any of the ethnic minorities and critics of the officer class as aberrant:

By making it clear that while Warden, Prewitt, and others might dislike their officers, this dislike stems from the realisation that they, as individuals, do not have the stuff to become officers … the officers might be placed in a better light.[36]

Adler and Taradash would smile and agree 'when we were with them. But we never intended to do it.'[37] After a four-hour meeting with Department of Defense heavies, Adler and Taradash realised, stunned and euphoric, that 'we were going to get everything we wanted without giving up much'.[38]

What they got was this: permission to shoot at Schofield Barracks and Hickham Field, old-style army uniforms for 400 men, 400 1903 Springfield rifles, twenty Thompson submachine guns, twenty Browning automatic rifles (BARs), fifteen 45-calibre pistols and 55,000 rounds of ammunition. Eight hundred soldiers from the Hawaiian Infantry Training Centre would appear in the film as extras. A group of planes from the 199th Squadron of the Hawaii Air National Guard participated in the reconstructed attacks on Pearl Harbor. Colonel Kendall Fielder and Warrant Officer William Mullen were allocated as technical advisors (but their 'advice' was confined to ensuring accuracy of uniforms and drill).

Having defeated the army in one meeting, Cohn, Adler and Taradash kept their heads down and guarded the contents of the script to avoid disruptive publicity. Jones's agent, Ned Brown, wrote his client that he 'tried my damnedest to get a copy of the treatment but it is so hush-hush that Adler could not let one out of his hands'.[39] Only after Christmas 1952 (when the cast and crew were almost ready to leave for Hawaii), did Adler finally send Jones the script. He liked it, but offered to make suggestions if the studio rehired him. Adler declined. But while Jones was waiting for the script back in New York, Norman Mailer had introduced him to his friend Montgomery Clift. 'I told Clift then, as I've always felt, he'd probably make a better Prewitt than just about anybody else I can think of.'[40] Although Cohn balked at hiring Clift, the young actor was better connected than Cohn realised. Fred Zinnemann, hired to direct in the spring of 1952, was one of Clift's closest friends.

Maggio (Frank Sinatra, standing lower left) warns Prewitt (Montgomery Clift) about life in the infantry at Schofield Barracks while cast and crew look on (BFI); off camera as Zinnemann works out the details of Prewitt's hazing with Claude Akins (Sergeant Dhom). (L–R) script supervisor Charlsie Bryant, assistant director Earl Bellamy, Jus Addiss, Zinnemann, Akins, Clift and Sinatra (AMPAS)

Taradash had just seen Zinnemann's work with newcomers Pier Angeli (*Teresa*, 1951) and Marlon Brando (*The Men*, 1950), and 'liked the way Zinnemann handled the GIs'.[41] He asked Adler to hire Zinnemann. Adler agreed enthusiastically and, though it was rumoured that Harry Cohn disliked Zinnemann's latest production *High Noon* (1952, shot on the Columbia Ranch), the soft-spoken European émigré was at the time the industry's most celebrated younger director. He had critical success with a number of war-themed films, among them *Act of Violence* (1948), and one of them, a European coproduction about child Holocaust survivors, *The Search* (1948), was very popular with audiences and critics and helped to make Montgomery Clift a major star. Zinnemann's first major A-feature, *The Seventh Cross* (1944), looked at prewar Germany's anti-Nazi resisters, and had a number of historical convergences with *From Here to Eternity*, including hunted loner-heroes and explicit scenes of police and military brutality. Zinnemann was interested in Adler's project, but cautious, writing: 'I don't want to commit myself until I'm sure that this can be a good picture … . Censorship may kill us.'[42] He was also wary of Cohn, who didn't want the picture to run over two hours and was ruthless in cutting the time he would allow directors and editors to put the final cut together. He had driven Taradash to fits of 'trembling' rage in his demands to cut the script to the bare bones. Cohn was equally wary of Zinnemann, one of the few directors to go on voluntary suspension early in his career at MGM because he disliked the poor scripts assigned to him. Cohn's comment, ' "I've got to have a director who I'm certain of" ', essentially meant he wanted a director whom he could boss around.[43] Zinnemann was not that type.

*High Noon*, in theatres at the time, was both a blessing and a curse for Zinnemann, personally and professionally. His friend Carl Foreman, who had written the script, was blacklisted and fled to England in 1952. An even closer friend, cinematographer Floyd Crosby, had been gray-listed and found it hard to obtain work, though Zinnemann had wanted him to photograph *From Here to Eternity*. There were charges in and outside Hollywood that *High*

*Noon* was anti-American in its critical view of the fabled US frontier, and Zinnemann's foreign and Jewish background hadn't helped disperse those accusations. He was understandably worried that taking on yet another film critical of American institutions would destroy his career.

Zinnemann had fallen out with Stanley Kramer during *High Noon* (Kramer had all but fired Crosby and had been unsupportive of Foreman, eventually forcing his resignation as coproducer), and had made his last picture for Kramer Productions, *Member of the Wedding* (1952), bitterly resentful of the producer. Kramer and associate George Glass tried to discourage Adler from hiring Zinnemann, saying behind his back that he was 'very difficult' and 'impossible to work with'.[44] But Taradash persevered; Zinnemann remained Columbia's only choice for director. With some persuading (and that seven-year, 2.5 per cent profit clause), he signed the contract. Like everyone else, Zinnemann had read *From Here to Eternity* with interest upon publication, but was a bit disappointed with the tone of Taradash's tough but humorous script. 'I miss the basic feeling of a peace-time, professional army. I believe that we must show the peace-time professional soldier as an outcast in an antagonistic world of civilians.'[45] He also felt that the caustic and cynical Warden from Jones's novel 'has lost much of his bite and aggressiveness' and privately noted in August, 'There is no indignation in this script. The quality of anger is gone. The temperature has cooled off – from boiling point to comfortably warm.'[46]

It was through Zinnemann's casting and his intense rehearsals with the actors, that the indignation and the anger of *Eternity* would return. He went through the book again, annotating and underlining, focusing on Prewitt's working-class backstory:

If at all possible, reference should be made to Prew's childhood – the fact that he was from Harlan County, Kentucky, that he grew up in the Depression – bummed all over the country and finally got into the army because 'he wasn't ready to starve yet'.[47]

He noted that Maggio's outspokenness and scapegoat status made him 'Red' and a 'Chaplin character'[48] (Charles Chaplin himself, whom Zinnemann met through their mutual friends Berthold and Salka Viertel, had just been thrown out of the US for alleged political offences). He was both intrigued and repelled by Karen's decision to remain with Holmes. Warden was a cipher. Zinnemann liked to cast against type and he liked getting his own way. But it was Adler who suggested that Lancaster play Warden and he agreed enthusiastically. Adler also suggested Alvin (Al) Sargent for a small role as Nair (the soldier shot by the Japanese), and years later Sargent met Zinnemann again – this time as the screenwriter of the director's current film, *Julia* (1977). Donna Reed had worked with Zinnemann before on the thriller *Eyes in the Night* (1942) but had never played a bad girl. But Zinnemann felt Reed had never reached her full potential, and playing a prostitute tended to enhance actresses' careers: Greta Garbo

An actor's director: Zinnemann (centre) with Clift and Sinatra (AMPAS)

(*Anna Christie*, 1930), Bette Davis (*Of Human Bondage*, 1934; *Marked Woman*, 1937), Joan Crawford (*Rain*, 1932), Marlene Dietrich (*The Blue Angel*, 1930) and Vivien Leigh (*Waterloo Bridge*, 1940) had been successful in variations of this role. Cohn had insisted on Joan Crawford as Karen, but as far as Zinnemann was concerned, she was only 'adequate'. Agent Bert Allenberg suggested his client Deborah Kerr, and the 'golden trio' (Adler, Zinnemann and Taradash) thought the casting of a 'chilly' lady to play the adulterous Karen Holmes would 'create an added sense of suspense and excitement'.[49] Eventually Crawford's insisting on hiring her personal cinematographer led to her losing the role to Kerr. If Zinnemann couldn't have Crosby, then no actress was going to have Burnett Guffey replaced. Additional auditions and casting were done in New York. It was there that they found many of Lorene's co-workers at the New Congress Club and Ernest Borgnine for the sadistic Sergeant Judson.

In 1976, *Julia*'s screenwriter Alvin Sargent gave Zinnemann this inscribed still: 'To my friend Fred Zinnemann, a great pilot – remembering the good old days – With affection, Alvin, August 1977'. Sargent played Nair (AMPAS)

Sinatra's fight to play Maggio is one of the best-known underdog stories of Hollywood casting, and was famously parodied by Mario Puzo and Francis Ford Coppola in *The Godfather* (1969, 1972). Many people have formed their picture of Columbia mogul Harry Cohn from the fictionalised Jack Woltz. Although the real Cohn did not sexually abuse child stars and the Mafia did not put a horse's head in his bed after he initially refused to give Frank Sinatra the part of Angelo Maggio, it is true that Cohn did not want Sinatra for the part. He wanted Eli Wallach, and Wallach allegedly made a riveting test. Some claim that Mrs Frank Sinatra, also known as Ava Gardner (*The Killers*; *Mogambo*, 1953), got Frank the part by going to Joan Cohn and talking woman-to-woman about the need to regenerate her husband's career (his vocal cords had haemorrhaged, and, as Taradash remembered, he 'was *really* flat on his rear').[50] It is very unlikely that this impassioned plea to Mrs Harry Cohn (or Cohn himself) changed the casting. But Wallach had a previous Broadway commitment to play in Tennessee Williams's *Camino Real* for Elia Kazan, and, according to Taradash, Cohn refused to pay Wallach double his original price as a way of changing his mind.

Zinnemann rarely agreed with Cohn about anything, but felt that he had been right about Wallach as Maggio. Zinnemann saw Maggio, even more than Prewitt, as the ultimate outsider: articulate, working class, even communist, and adding Wallach's Jewishness into the mix of contexts would have darkened Maggio's brutal eradication from the American military in 1953. But eventually, Zinnemann adjusted to Sinatra. The actor was playing the part

Sinatra, reading *Variety* in Maggio's fatigues, parodies his low-rent career as a fallen star. Things would change in August when *From Here to Eternity* opened (AMPAS)

for a pittance ($8,000), but completely focused on his role and utterly professional on the set. The actor's initially good relationship with Clift would make rehearsals and shooting enjoyable for Zinnemann, although their titanic drinking bouts with visiting celebrity author James Jones made things more difficult. Cohn eventually reconciled himself to losing Wallach, and even became friends with Sinatra after the production wrapped. (It helped that later on Sinatra did him the occasional favour in his Las Vegas shows to boost a Columbia picture's exhibition potential).

But Cohn hadn't wanted Clift for Prewitt either (largely because he knew Clift was bisexual). His other casting ideas, which included Aldo Ray (*Pat and Mike*, 1952) for Prewitt and Broderick Crawford (*All the President's Men*, 1949) for Warden, were overridden by Zinnemann and Adler. In fact, Zinnemann told Cohn flatly that he would walk away from the project altogether if Cohn didn't sign Clift: ' "If you want another actor, you'd better get another director" ',[51] he said quietly, leaving Cohn screaming at him in his empty office. Cohn sent Clift the script the next day, however. Zinnemann said of Cohn: 'We started our working relationship on the basis of mutual hatred, mixed with mutual respect'.[52] Ever since the director and Clift had made *The Search* in Europe, they had been looking for another project on which they could collaborate. As Clift wrote Zinnemann in 1948:

I told [Arthur Loew] the three of us ought to work together sometime and soon. Now it's up to some untalented author to give us a reason to get together. Why aren't authors as talented as you and I? All authors are nudnicks.[53]

Zinnemann didn't get close to people easily, but 'Monty' could tease Zinnemann about his growing celebrity status as a director, he adored Zinnemann's son Tim and often dropped in unannounced at their Santa Monica house for dinner. Zinnemann thought he would never find another actor with Clift's artistry, honesty and willingness

to take risks, and tolerated Clift's worsening drinking problem and insecurities. As he stated in a rare interview with Hedda Hopper,

Monty and I get along fine because we think alike ... . When he comes to me with suggestions, I'm ready to listen, because I respect him. He goes very deeply into whatever character he portrays, and is able to project truthfully. Sometimes I think he doesn't act at all. He behaves as the character would.[54]

With Zinnemann and Clift on the project, Adler needed all his diplomatic skills to keep Cohn from going after the script, his

As Zinnemann looks on, military advisors show Clift how to strip down and reassemble his rifle (AMPAS)

Crew shot. Burnett Guffey and Zinnemann sit on one side, assistant cameraman Bob Uhl and camera operator Frank 'Kit' Carson are on the other. Charlsie Bryant holds the script; Burt Lancaster plays the star in sunglasses (AMPAS)

director and his star. Normally the head of a studio would not involve himself so closely on an individual production. In the past, Cohn had left details of individual films to his line producers, but he was not only appallingly rude to Adler, held three (usually pointless) preproduction meetings per week about the script and made disruptive appearances on location in Hawaii, but he also allowed his name to be put on advertisements for the film – a first in his company's history. Yet, in spite of his almost daily bouts with Taradash and Zinnemann, most of Cohn's creative choices for the film – with the standout exception of the two-hour running time – were abandoned. When shooting started in Hawaii, as Zinnemann remembered, 'Typically, Cohn had demanded shooting to begin upon arrival after the night flight from Los Angeles, but we just didn't do it'.[55]

They also began the production at the studio with five days of rehearsal (covering the material at the New Congress Club and at Lorene's house) beginning Monday 2 March 1953, and only started shooting on Saturday the 7th.[56] This suited Clift and Reed's style, as they both enjoyed developing their work; Sinatra, as Zinnemann revealed, instead did his best on the first take. 'It was an interesting problem … how to get their best performances from them in the same take.'[57] Even with such a tight shooting schedule (forty-one days), Zinnemann was able to get another week of rehearsal in Los Angeles from Tuesday 17 to Saturday 21 March. By the time the company flew out to Hawaii on 13 April, they had shot everything they needed on the lot. The cast stayed at the Alexander Young Hotel and began shooting Prewitt's arrival at Schofield on Wednesday 15 April. Petite and meticulous Charlsie Bryant acted as continuity girl, keeping Adler (whom she had known for years at MGM) abreast of their work and acting as yet another buffer for Zinnemann. Zinnemann liked minimal distractions so he could work closely with his actors, but it was difficult on a film that attracted as much publicity as *From Here to Eternity*. In addition to the visits from military dignitaries and last-minute disturbances from Cohn (the company remained in Hawaii until 3 May), Magnum Studio

photographers would be at the beach to shoot stills for *Look*, independent photographer Bob Willoughby had appeared to do some 'artistic' shots of Zinnemann directing and the ubiquitous still photographers were snapping away, catching Zinnemann in close conference with Reed, Kerr, Lancaster, Clift and Sinatra. Zinnemann had a tendency to speak very quietly and close up to his actors, making the off-camera narrative archived in still shots almost as interesting as the film itself. Always the Hollywood outsider, he would need all his reputed stubbornness and commitment to the material to win his confrontations with Harry Cohn.

✳ ✳ ✳

The credits roll as the soldiers count their steps and move across the screen. The camera pans with them briefly, then pauses at a crossroads. Dead centre, in the distance, a lone figure saunters into

Charlsie Bryant takes off her sunglasses to write down some of Buddy Adler's notes (AMPAS)

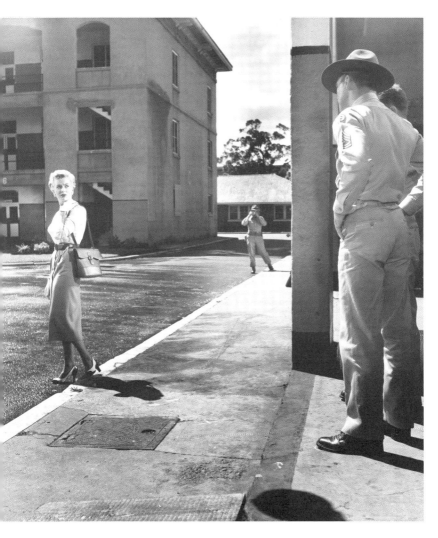

As Kerr, Mickey Shaughnessy (Leva) and Lancaster pose for Irving Lippman, a soldier from Schofield Barracks takes some personal photos (AMPAS)

the foreground: neat, khakied and, as Jones had first described him, 'deceptively slim'. As the man moves closer, George Duning's score is complicated with a slow, southern, minor blues strain, moving in counterpoint to the marching men. The soldier carries his gear over his shoulder, cap tilted slightly in the early morning heat. He is seen clearly for a moment in a break between the marching platoons; Adler and Zinnemann's credits are stamped over his image with a kind of finality. But the subsequent intertitle, 'Schofield Barracks, Hawaii, 1941', loads the historical dice. How many days to Pearl Harbor? How many days does that man, or any of the marching soldiers, have left before the Japanese attack on 7 December? His steps slow slightly as he waits for the last platoon to move out of his way and, as he turns, the camera moves toward him into a low-angle close-up before panning along with him. It's our first look at Robert E. Lee Prewitt, who, even as he approaches his new posting, moves against the established space of the shot, crossing the army's horizontal movement, and recentring our gaze on him.

Yes or no? Fred Zinnemann seems momentarily unsure of how to answer Moana Gleason (Rose) (AMPAS)

Against the grain: Prewitt arrives at Schofield Barracks; the camera moves into a close-up

Zinnemann had used a similar set-up to introduce Robert Ryan's avenging GI Joe Parkson in *Act of Violence*, when he tracked down the ex-commanding officer Enley (Van Heflin) who had betrayed his own men in a Nazi-run prisoner-of-war camp. Parkson has to wait while a parade of prosperous, overweight 'patriots' march down Main Street in the town where Enley has become a successful businessman and public figure. Both Ryan and Clift's outsider protagonists spend a lot of their screentime defending their own sense of truth and justice in the face of mainstream American compromise and corruption. Later in life, Zinnemann liked drawing attention to these linked visual touches across his work. Clift's long walk toward the camera is undoubtedly well worth the wait. After he starred with Elizabeth Taylor in George Stevens's *A Place in the Sun* (1951), Clift had been widely publicised as one of Hollywood's most gifted actors and handsomest men. Zinnemann appreciated his close friend's appeal to both men and women; a few minutes later, Milt Warden and Sergeant Leva (Mickey Shaughnessy) wait for sexy army wife Karen Holmes to approach them in a near-replay of the set-up used to introduce Prewitt!

But while Warden will stare bleakly at Prewitt with measuring cynicism, Private Angelo Maggio is frankly delighted to see his old friend turning up to break the monotony of his work detail, though he's utterly bewildered why 'Prew' would quit a cushy job in the Bugle Corps for Captain Holmes's infantry outfit. Maggio, who's been picking up cigarette butts outside the company commander's office in his fatigues, spits out in a marked Hoboken accent, 'This outfit they can give back to General Custer'. Later he will say other unflattering things about the outfit before Sergeant 'Fatso' Judson beats the life out of him in the stockade. For now, Prew nods noncommittally and moves inside to 'look around'.

*From Here to Eternity* is often epitomised by fans and critics as the kiss-on-the-beach film, or one of the more adult-themed 1950s films to showcase adultery and prostitution via the heterosexual relationships of Karen and Warden and Lorene and Prewitt. But the

Karen moves into the frame, occupying the dead space in front of Warden and Leva; 'You quit the Bugle Corps?' Maggio does not think much of his friend's decision to join Holmes's company

friendship between Prew and Maggio is arguably more poignant than any of the film's more traditional romantic couplings. It isn't just that Sinatra and Clift gave the performances of their careers in this film. Both actors were able to convey the honest and unflinching bond that exists between two men who share a profession, a sense of humour and an outlook on life. Wise-cracking Angelo Maggio will stand up for his friend throughout his abusive 'treatment' at the hands of the company boxers, and will often get kicked for his pains. Likewise, late in the film, Prewitt stands by Maggio and kills his murderer, knowing that it will mean the end of his army career and even his life. But in these opening moments, Zinnemann keeps them in a series of low-key, companionable two-shots.

Sinatra, though known primarily as a singer, had been in films before (*Anchors Aweigh*, 1945; *Take Me Out to the Ball Game*, 1949; *On the Town*, 1949 – all co-starring Gene Kelly), but it was usually to display his voice and mega-kilowatt smile. In an interview published shortly after the film's New York release, the actor would claim: ' "The part was made to order for me. I knew hundreds of Maggios in Hoboken where I was brought up. And I came close to becoming one myself" '.[58] Sinatra's playfulness and almost intense geniality work well with Clift's more emotionally spare approach to Prewitt in the opening sequences. But while Sinatra chose to inflect his role with the Brooklyn-Hoboken accent of his youth, the southern-born Clift chose not to use a Kentucky accent for Prewitt, despite getting records of Harlan County, Kentucky speech to study with Zinnemann.[59]

Prewitt and Maggio may be from polar opposite backgrounds (white, southern, agrarian/Harlan County mining for Prew; ethnic, urban for Maggio), but they are both working-class recruits, thirty-year enlisted men, and not from the officer class. In Jones's novel, Prewitt's Uncle John Turner had served in the Spanish-American War and in the Philippines, but his father and uncle were both casualties of different wars – Harlan County mine strikes in 1919. Although Prewitt's working-class history didn't make it to Taradash's final

Warden surveys Prewitt; Prewitt surveys Warden

script, Zinnemann and Clift were deeply drawn to his backstory and Clift played his version of the underdog in close solidarity with Maggio's ethnic soldier. From the beginning, we learn that Prewitt is stubborn. As we soon discover, it's earned him a certain reputation on the base. But as we also learn from watching him shoot pool alone in the rec room, he does everything easily, skilfully and with unselfconscious perfection. He sinks one ball and aims for another before looking up at 'topkick' First Sergeant Milton Warden.

Burt Lancaster at the time was Hollywood's top male star. He had made the transition from innovative producer Mark Hellinger's film noirs to popular action films, and had even starred as Sergeant Mike Kincaid of the French Foreign Legion in *Ten Tall Men* (1951). The role obviously set him up to be cast as Warden ('this *was* type-casting', Zinnemann acknowledged), and Lancaster would continue to play memorable granite-faced tough guys throughout his career (*The Train*, 1964; *The Professionals*, 1966; *Castle Keep*, 1969). Lancaster came out of East Harlem, New York City, with a background to suit Milt Warden's hard cold stares. Zinnemann contrasts Maggio and Prewitt's scenes with the stark shot/reverse shot, medium close-up standoff between Warden and Prewitt in the poolroom. But though Warden, 'with the enormous self-assurance which makes him very quiet' (Zinnemann's notes)[60] growls that he's 'heard about you', Prewitt doesn't miss a beat, retorting, with some gentle humour: 'I've heard about you too, Sergeant'. In that moment, not only two types of soldiers and men, but also two types of actors, were taking each other's measure.

Warden may be the First Sergeant or 'topkick' of the company, but he's *not* an officer (as he will later yell at Karen Holmes when she urges him to take an officer training course: 'I hate officers. I've always hated officers'). He's an enlisted man, and may once have been a cannier version of Prewitt, joining the Depression-era peacetime army like many others because he didn't want to starve and was looking for a profession. But we don't ever really learn anything about Warden in the course of the film, apart from the fact that he is a model First Sergeant. He's a smart, diplomatic manager, and a soldier who once distinguished himself in combat in the Pacific. The army suits Warden perfectly. Like Warden, Lancaster was determined to rise in the ranks of his profession. He was always trying to learn as much as he could from each project, and often annoyed directors by asking to change his lines. He wanted control, and made an early move to independent producing with Harold Hill and Ben Hecht. His energy was legendary, and two years after his Oscar-nominated performance as Warden, he would bring home the Best Picture award for *Marty* (1955), with *Eternity* co-star Ernest Borgnine in the title role. But Lancaster's work as an actor was not accorded the critical respect that Clift's received. By a few accounts, Clift didn't like Lancaster, and thought he was no actor and ' "the most unctuous man I've ever met" '.[61] Lancaster gave a candid interview about Clift: ' "He approached the script like a scientist … . The only time I was ever really afraid as an actor was that first scene with Clift … I was afraid he was going to blow me right off the screen." '[62] But these compliments aside, Lancaster may have grown tired of Clift's irresponsible off-the-set behaviour. While in Hawaii, he often had to carry the dead-drunk Clift and Sinatra back to their hotels and put them to bed, actions which allegedly earned him Christmas cards from Sinatra addressed 'To Mom'.[63]

Clift when sober may have posed a threat to Lancaster's star status, so the older actor's defence was to play Warden with coiled power and a menacing smile. And this was Zinnemann's key to recovering the 'anger' he felt the script lacked. We may not learn anything definite about Warden, but he is seething. He may be able to turn the rage on and off in the course of the film, but it's a tension that is only just held in check. There is *no* trouble in his company, and Prewitt is *nothing but* trouble. Somebody will have to change, and it won't be Warden. Warden is there to stop Prewitt from enjoying himself 'before sundown' and, for a while it seems, at any other time, and he manoeuvres Prewitt into the first of many confrontations with his new company commander, Captain Dana

Holmes. It's clear from the outset who really runs this company.
Warden barely tolerates the slow Mazzioli (Harry Bellaver) and
incompetent and sloppy Leva, and treats his vain and greedy
company commander with a mixture of faked respectful deference
and bland contempt. Lancaster moves beautifully through the scene,
orchestrating the space. He manages all of the disparate personalities
and elements in G Company, but may have met his match with
Prewitt. Seated and waiting, Prewitt may seem under Warden's
control, but Maggio, speaking from the window screen in another
two-shot, restarts the conversation with Prew, injecting his usual
irreverence and kinship of the underdog: 'You're the best bugler they
got on this whole island … I feel for you, pal, but in my position I just
can't reach you'. Prew grins up at Maggio, but wipes it effortlessly as
Warden sweeps by, cutting into the two-shot.

Captain Holmes's role caused Buddy Adler and Daniel
Taradash more difficulties than any other character in the script. He

Maggio's smart-alec commentary and Zinnemann's framing keep the two friends
together

represented the officer corps at its most arrogant, corrupt and inept. Holmes's real interest in his army career is in managing his company boxers and winning the end-of-year sports trophy he hopes will earn him a promotion from General Slater (Fay Roope). 'Every boxer in this outfit's a non-com', Corporal Buckley (Jack Warden) warns Prewitt later that night. Holmes does nothing of the day-to-day management of the company, and instead runs around with hatcheck girls and oversees the brutal hazing of Prewitt. At the end of Jones's novel, Holmes is promoted. This was something Taradash knew 'would be ruinous if we tried to cope with it'.[64] The army felt that showing Holmes being punished by military officials would make him look like the one rotten apple in the barrel, but they were forgetting that Holmes and his non-com boxers are the officers we see almost exclusively in the course of the film. Philip Ober's performance is spot on; he looks like an officer: big, beefy and confident, but he is also false, calculating and incompetent.

Zinnemann and set designer Frank Tuttle designed the company commander's offices in a series of tiered, semi-open rooms. As Holmes examines Prewitt for the first time, Mazzioli's lowly clerk's office is seen in the background, Warden's office mid-ground and then Holmes's desk at the end, facing the subordinates. Warden hovers in the mid-ground with paperwork, casting sly glances at Prewitt's back, listening to the interview, waiting to strike. It is Holmes who reads Prewitt's service record/biography; born in Kentucky, he is a southerner who enlisted at Fort Myers, Virginia, and rose to be First Bugler. Holmes reveals that he snapped up Prewitt's transfer because he remembered one of Prewitt's impressive middleweight matches the previous year. As he makes his 'pitch' to Prewitt, Warden smirks. When Prewitt tries to deflect Holmes's question about what trouble caused him to transfer, Warden, with a touch of officer theatricals, slams a filing cabinet shut; there are no 'personal matters' for this sergeant, and indeed while the four other protagonists (Lorene, Karen, Maggio and Prewitt) each narrate extensive personal stories about their pasts later in the film, Warden

does not. Aside from some brief comments later from Corporal Buckley about Warden's action in the Philippines ('He's the best soldier I ever saw'), we learn nothing about his past life. It's to Lancaster's credit that on screen Warden is more than just a cardboard cutout of military perfection.

On cue, Holmes lets Warden's polished interrogation proceed. Warden conducts it like a military manoeuvre. He begins questioning Prewitt at the private's back, before moving forward for a frontal assault. Prewitt tells them with great reluctance about the topkick who replaced him with a new 'friend' as the company's First Bugler, and Warden sniffs in contempt: 'His feelings were hurt'. Holmes tries circling him too, and Prewitt admits that he gave up boxing when one of his punches hurt another boxer, a fellow southerner, Dixie Wells. Holmes is unmoved and reminds Prewitt that 'it's not the individual that counts' in the army. But of course, this is typical managerial self-serving bullshit: the whole confrontation happens because of

The spatial hierarchies of the set design (seated, Philip Ober as Captain Holmes)

Holmes's personal career needs. Throughout both interrogations, Prewitt remains stationary, looking straight ahead of him and finally, Holmes leaves, fed up, to go into 'town' to see a prostitute, or possibly, given traditional army moral codes, the wife of a fellow officer. Warden knows this code, but remains polite until the screen door slams off screen. 'He'd strangle on his own spit if he didn't have me there to swab his throat out for him', he remarks out of the side of his mouth to no one in particular. He turns slightly over his right shoulder to see Prewitt looking at him, puzzled at the First Sergeant's obvious contempt for his commanding officer, a contempt beyond even Maggio's barbed comments about the company. Warden thaws, ever so slightly, and tells Prewitt to follow him.

Outside the barracks, Warden, hands on his hips, doesn't try to convince Prewitt of anything. But after five years in the army, 'Isn't it about time you got smart?' he asks the younger man. They face each other, Prewitt balancing his heavy kit bags and Warden balancing his First Sergeant's hat. As Warden explains the way Holmes's company works and why Prewitt will do what he says to make Warden's life easier, he moves like a boxer, keeping his chin down, looking at Prewitt carefully from under his brows, turning, walking, pausing, to control the conversation, to make his point. Prew is silent during these manoeuvres, and his contained remark, 'I can soldier with any man', seems to silence Warden for the moment. This is no prima donna bugler, Warden realises, but someone who bears more watching.

But at that moment, Warden is distracted by the arrival of Karen Holmes in her light-coloured convertible. Deborah Kerr, in newly bleached-blonde hair and figure-skimming skirt and sweater, is worth a stare. Kerr was a surprise as the cheating army wife for more than Harry Cohn (who had wanted the more obvious Crawford), and not just because she was the only 'foreign' actor in the cast. Zinnemann particularly felt Kerr's ambivalent star status was an asset; audiences really wondered if she slept around, whereas, he commented, 'with all due respect, if you looked at Joan Crawford,

you wouldn't find it impossible to believe she sleeps with everybody'.[65] Born in Glasgow, Kerr switched careers from dancing to acting as a young girl and went on to become Michael Powell's muse in *The Life and Death of Colonel Blimp* (1942) and *Black Narcissus* (1947). MGM bought her contract and Kerr subsequently starred in a number of high-profile melodramas and historical romps, including *Edward, My Son* (1949) with Spencer Tracy, *The Prisoner of Zenda* (1952) as Princess Flavia, and as King Henry's last wife Catherine Parr in the biopic *Young Bess* (1953). But she had lost some of the momentum from her years as a British star, and seemed destined to become a younger replacement for the studio's resident redhead and rather boring pillar of British virtue, Greer Garson (*Mrs. Miniver*, 1942; *Mrs. Parkington*, 1944). *From Here to Eternity* would not only change her hair colour (Powell would complain about Kerr's 'upsetting' transformation into a bleach-blonde Hollywood bombshell), but also Kerr's range as an actress and status

Taking each other's measure, on and off the set

as a major international star. As Kerr wrote in 1953, 'I was thrilled when I was asked to play the part. … It makes me a glamorous, exciting woman – so different from the parts I've had in the past.'[66] Playing Karen liberated Kerr. She would go on to face Robert Mitchum (*Heaven Knows, Mr. Allison*, 1957), David Niven (*Separate Tables*, 1958; *Bonjour, Tristesse*, 1958) and Cary Grant (*An Affair to Remember*, 1957) in some of the biggest box-office hits of the 1950s. Kerr's rumoured relationship with Fred Zinnemann made things interesting on the set of *From Here to Eternity* (and may have been another reason for Powell's chagrin and Cohn telling Renée Zinnemann her husband 'is a louse'), but the two would remain on close terms through their work in Australia on *The Sundowners* (1960) and Kerr's marriage to Zinnemann's longtime friend, Peter Viertel, that year.

Despite her white gloves, there was no trace of the proper British lady in Kerr's characterisation of Karen. She is married to what she doesn't want (as Taradash laughed: 'Why she would marry this guy, I don't know'),[67] but being the company commander's wife gives her a certain amount of power. Her own consciousness of her physical power and a certain amount of glacial confidence were some compensation for a barren marriage. She drives onto the base as if she owns it. 'This place is getting to be like the Royal Hawaiian Hotel', snarls Warden, and Prew, starstruck, merely asks: 'Who is *that*?' Well, so much for Kerr's rather dowdy, good-girl British look of the 1940s! All the Hollywood movie stars used to stay at the Royal Hawaiian before and after the war, but high-end prostitutes used to meet their clients there as well, and Warden's remark conflates both Kerr's stardom as an on-location movie star and military men's contempt for all women on the masculine territory of the barracks (particularly one as confident as Karen). Warden avoids speaking with her, intent on re-educating Prewitt, and she walks purposefully into the commander's office, swinging her handbag in the distance.

The two men stroll while Warden talks ('You'll box, Prewitt; you'll box because Captain Holmes wants to be Major Holmes'), but

Zinnemann and Kerr strolling on the boardwalk at Waikiki while the tourists look on (AMPAS)

Prewitt finally stops and turns, framed by the barracks, looking coolly and levelly at Warden. 'I know where I stand. A man don't go his own way is nothing', he drawls softly (as Zinnemann noted in his script, 'not sophisticated, aggressive, not passive, tense, on edge, belligerent'), but his words are as steely as those of the first Kentuckian, Daniel Boone. In reverse shot, Warden concedes: 'Maybe in the days of the pioneers a man could go his own way, but today you've got to play ball'. American masculinity and old-fashioned frontier individuality have been replaced, ironically with an expression drawn from British imperial discourse. Play the game, compromise, fit into the system – or else. Prewitt's southern name and western heritage are out of date in 1941.

But these frontier references, drawn from Jones's novel, give *From Here to Eternity* resonance with the Western film genre. Both Lancaster and Clift had made their names in Westerns: Clift's first film work was in *Red River* (1948) opposite the legendary John Wayne, and Lancaster played a rancher in *Vengeance Valley* (1951). Hollywood played on Lancaster's urban roots early in his career, casting him as a succession of sympathetic crooks and confidence men but, after *From Here to Eternity*, he transitioned into Westerns (*Vera Cruz*, 1954; *The Kentuckian*, 1955; *The Professionals*), and he even played a sympathetic Native American (in full redface and rawhide) in *Apache* (1954). Hollywood film-makers liked to experiment with the Western genre, and there were a number of Westerns set in the twentieth century or in the US's post-frontier Pacific empire (of which Hawaii had been part since 1893), which engaged with issues of racism and expansion and frontier destiny (*Cimarron*, 1931; *Pancho Villa*, 1934; *The Real Glory*, 1939; *Viva Zapata!*, 1952). But *From Here to Eternity* also explores the tension between class and power animating many Western cavalry narratives: for every Western about a famous but vain and incompetent officer such as General George Armstrong Custer (John Ford's *Fort Apache*, released in 1948, stands out in this context), there were ten about nameless, unknown men like Prewitt who came out of nowhere to do

things their way and build a nation. This, to a certain extent, echoes
Frederick Jackson Turner's famous frontier thesis: the uniqueness of
the American experience out West was its alleged democratising
environment and elimination of class distinctions. (Prewitt's own
uncle, John Turner (note the surname!) believed in this ideology when
he headed west with Pershing's army.[68] But perhaps the most famous
Western, *Stagecoach* (1939), pointed out the persistence of class
prejudice on the frontier. It persists in *From Here to Eternity*'s more
modern America, too.

Warden barks at the dumpy supply clerk, who is eating an apple
and typing with the other hand. Italian-American Leva, unlike the
cringing Mazzioli, barks back, complaining, as every soldier does,
about the lousy pay in the army. It's interesting to note how many
Italian Americans are in the film's peacetime army; Maggio isn't
made the typical ethnic outsider scapegoat, despite army demands
in conferences with Adler and Taradash that he be singled out as a
failure. With Prew off to stow his gear, Leva and Warden stand by
the curb, off centre, backs to the frame, looking off toward the
commander's office. It's an unusual set-up and framing choice. Half
the frame's foreground is dead space. Then Karen appears in long
shot as she leaves the commander's office and walks toward them.
They don't acknowledge her; they don't move; they don't smile. It
would be a difficult walk for any woman under the stares of two such
men, but Karen manages it by looking 'colder than an iceberg',
despite Leva's barrack-room gossip that 'she knows the score, like
I've been telling you', and has been cuckolding her husband with a
variety of men over several years.

Kerr walks firmly toward them, stopping in medium close-up,
taking over the empty space on the other side of the frame. She has
allegedly come in for 'some things' her husband was to have left for
her, thereby turning the base into a wider domestic space that she
dominates (with Warden, by implication, one of her domestics). But
Warden responds, deadpan, that he's in town (pause) 'on business'.
They both know what this phrase really means, and share the open

secret of Holmes's professional incompetence and philandering. But Warden knows about her husband's sexual failure with his wife and advances, asking her 'If there's anything *I* can do?', before then following up with: 'I'd like to help, ma'am'. Karen turns, half-smiling over her shoulder, in a pretty medium 'come-on' close-up. But this is not a woman who's going to be objectified or looked at without consequences. The camera holds, and she walks fearlessly into a tighter close-up, her eyes looking him over closely, carefully, with practice, and without any desire to please. With a mixture of half-interest and amused contempt, she begins to interrogate him in much the same way Holmes and Warden questioned Prewitt. 'My husband's told me a lot about you, Sergeant. He says you're very efficient.' Warden, with faked meekness, agrees, and then explains that he was 'born smart'. She smiles, but not with her eyes, and turns her back on them. Leva, exhaling from the tension, remarks that 'she sure is one' but Warden, realising that he may not have come out on top in this verbal war between the sexes, snarls that he's 'seen better'. Leva, sharing his two-shot, looks over at his chief with raised eyebrows, disbelieving.

Karen isn't like other 'wives' seen in studio-era Hollywood films. Jean Harlow may have sassed them right back (*Platinum Blonde*, 1931; *Bombshell*, 1933), Barbara Stanwyck may have two-timed with the best of them (*The Lady Eve*, 1941; *Double Indemnity*, 1944) and Katharine Hepburn may have treated them with the contempt they occasionally deserved (*The Philadelphia Story*, 1940; *Adam's Rib*, 1949), but Kerr's performance has few precedents, aside from Lauren Bacall's bored divorcée Vivian Rutledge in *The Big Sleep* (1946). Nor is Karen a 'desperate housewife' variety more in fashion in the postmodern 'nostalgic' return to 1950s themes (*Far from Heaven*, 2005; *Mad Men*, AMC, 2007–; *Desperate Housewives*, ABC, 2004–12). She smokes before bed, and uses smoking as a tough-gal prop when she hears Holmes return. She brushes her hair purposefully, without preening, avoids looking at her husband, and tells him to 'get out of my bedroom' with deadpan finality. This lady

Karen, mildly interested, looks back at Warden

Not your typical close-up

So you've really seen better? Leva looks sceptically at his topkick

doesn't scream, doesn't make scenes and doesn't cry. She also doesn't like her husband, and is a cool, bland audience for his 'office' complaints. She listens to his lies about whom he was seeing in Kaneohe and just doesn't give a damn. She only enjoys catching him in lies about his adulterous 'business' because 'I want you to know that I'm not as stupid as you maintain all women are'. It's one of the film's many frank and surprising scenes, frank in its revelations about masculine contempt for women, women's awareness of this contempt and their completely reciprocated feelings. But it's also a telling commentary upon marriage as it was not only in 1953 but also potentially in the early 1940s, when the film was set. Divorces were on the rise from the 1920s, with plenty of marriages failing due to poverty and unemployment in the Depression (women often kept secretarial positions while men lost their heavy-industry jobs). By 1940, the percentage of divorces out of the total number of marriages had reached 20 per cent, and in the early 1950s (after a postwar divorce spike), divorces had again risen to 25 per cent.[69] The backlash against married women wanting something outside the home was growing (read almost any page of Philip Wylie's *Generation of Vipers*, 1942), and despite more open discussions of female sexuality, women were receiving a number of ambivalent signals from the media about what they should be.[70]

One 'domestic' scene is followed by another, but no less problematic. A smoky establishing shot of the rec room shows Prew and Maggio playing a game of pool at the end of the day. The rest of the company is relaxing; even Warden is playing solitaire in the foreground, seated in splendid isolation at his own small table. But the film cuts to a reverse angle as the company boxers exchange looks and abandon their poker game. Warden, in close-up, looks up swiftly, aware that Prewitt's 'treatment' is about to begin. Gradually the camera moves closer to Prewitt, increasing the sense of something closing in on him. Prewitt doesn't miss a shot, but he has to squeeze past one non-com in close-up and the smoke and tension increase as Ike Galovitch (John Dennis) lays it on the line: He may say he won't

box, but 'out in the field' they will make him 'sing a different tune'. Maggio tells them to 'take off', and the space opens up alongside the pool table, but Galovitch's threats again set the camera on a close-up of Prewitt. Clift stands up straight from a shot and tells them flat-out that he quit fighting, and that 'if you guys want to put the screws on, go right ahead; I can take anything you can dish out'. This is the first time Prewitt has raised his voice and his pale eyes are blazing. Although Warden may treat him with wary dislike, as a bomb that might explode and make him more paperwork, as Prewitt, Clift indicates he will only explode if he's shaken the wrong way. They retreat, but Prewitt doesn't want to play pool any more. As the non-coms and Prewitt disperse, the shot reframes on Maggio, who has been watching his friend and is angry. 'I just hate to see a good guy get it in the gut', he explains to Corporal Buckley, as Buckley puts up his cue. Buckley's remark – 'You better get used to it, kid; you'll probably see a lot of it before you die' – is one of many prophetic

As newspaper headlines warn of the impending war, Dhom and his non-com boxer cronies Thornhill (Robert Karnes), Henderson (Robert Wilke), Galovitch (John Dennis) and Wilson (Douglas Henderson) prepare to haze Prewitt

lines in the film. Maggio, like Prewitt, will resist hazing and abuse to the death, literally dying from his beating in the stockade some months later. Taradash was also extremely clever here: while during army negotiations, officials had hoped to persuade Columbia 'the flag ought to be waved more'[71] and show that Maggio and Prewitt deserved what they got, here Taradash indicates that hazing and abuse in the army are quite common: Maggio's going to see a lot of it – precisely because he has made a career in the military.

Though *From Here to Eternity* is ostensibly about the work and personal lives of people in the last days before Pearl Harbor, the army also functions as a character, seldom heroic, very complicated, bureaucratic and corrupt. We see it from a distance and too close. Though Zinnemann was already known for his penchant for close-ups (*The Seventh Cross*; *High Noon*), his use of deep focus and composition-in-depth served to reinforce the critical edge of Taradash's script. Cinematographer Gregg Toland had been the first to develop these techniques in Hollywood and was an important influence on Zinnemann as well as a close friend until his early death in 1948. As Zinnemann used Toland's reconstructed Pearl Harbor attack shots from *December 7th*, Toland could also be credited as co-cinematographer on *From Here to Eternity*. Zinnemann and Burnett Guffey use a lot of deep-focus set-ups throughout the film and, within the first fifteen minutes, Prewitt's opening scene, Karen's first meeting with Warden and the office interrogation all combine deep-focus with close-ups, often within a single shot. They continue to employ this approach later as 'Taps' signals the end of Prewitt's first day in Company G. While Buckley privately warns Prewitt about how bad 'the treatment' can be when the non-commissioned officers gang up on one man, Maggio gets ready for bed and another soldier next to Prewitt quietly reads Walt Whitman's *Leaves of Grass* (a favourite of Zinnemann's), reminding us again that Prewitt's spiritual freedom is something that cannot be suppressed. Prew listens to Buckley but, as the lights go out, he turns away from the close-up, pulling the covers over his shoulders.

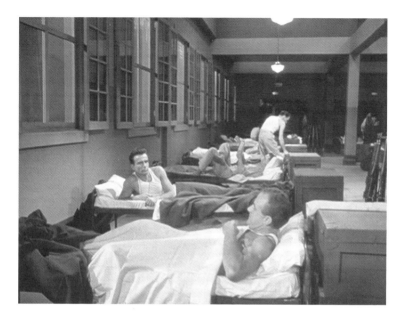

The next morning, 'the treatment' begins. A high-angle
establishing long shot of drilling soldiers, ironically drawn from
a magazine photo Zinnemann had found in the months before
shooting, makes the most of the Hawaii location shots, extras and
military equipment acquired through Adler's cordial relationship
with Washington. It seems like a good advertisement for the US army
(possibly even good recruiting for the Korean War), but is followed
by less pretty scenes, some of which Warden watches from above in
the barracks. Claude Akins's Dhom, and later Thornhill (Robert
Karnes) and Henderson (Robert Wilke), single-out Prewitt from
the unit for allegedly not being in step during drill (a lie), having the
rear sight off in assembling the rifle (Prewitt is first to assemble his
rifle, and then Thornhill deliberately unscrews the rear sight and
misaligns it) and falling during combat drills (he's tripped). A native
Kentuckian like the famed World War I hero Sergeant Alvin York
(played by Gary Cooper in *Sergeant York*, 1941), Prewitt knows his

Corporal Buckley (Jack Warden, foreground) warns Prewitt about 'the treatment'

rifle better than any man there, but never shows the slightest emotion under 'the treatment' (which York, initially even as a conscientious objector in World War I, does not face from his fellow soldiers).

But the film balances the abuse and heavier, more adult themes with comedy. From the first, Zinnemann had seen Maggio as a 'Chaplin character', and Maggio's honest outrage and reactions to the system articulate the audience's and any outsider's response to 'the treatment', but honesty comes with a price. When he goes after Henderson for tripping Prewitt: 'Are you crazy? I saw what you did!', Zinnemann immediately cuts to a two-shot of the friends running together around the track with their rifles raised in the burning sun. Maggio is a stand-in for the audience; we see what he sees and share his outrage. Taradash had resisted any army attempts to make Maggio look like a loser who got what he deserved. The army officials seemed to have it in for Maggio's character even more than Prewitt. In the novel, Prewitt and Maggio are both drawn to a soldier

The army in long shot looks impressive

Up close, it is far less pleasant. Anderson gloats at the fallen Prewitt while Maggio looks on, outraged; together again. Maggio joins Prewitt for punishment laps

in the stockade called Jack Malloy. Malloy is a communist and manages to escape the stockade, but not before honing a lot of Maggio's anti-establishment feeling.

If Maggio and Warden are the two on the military's blacklist, then Warden, the one protagonist who will survive and remain in Hawaii to fight the 'Good War', is one of the silent majority too careful to speak out. In this first 'treatment' sequence, Warden is seen from above, silently watching the hazing. But in the next scene, he's also watching Karen as she drives by with a smile in her convertible. While no one gets on Warden's case for watching and not doing anything for Prewitt, Leva, gobbling a candy bar, remonstrates with the chief: 'Keep your mind off what you're thinking; what do you want to do, wind up in Leavenworth?' Warden's slow turn and bleak stare in profile at the dumpy Leva are comically reminiscent of Scarlett (Vivien Leigh) and Mammy (Hattie McDaniel) in *Gone with the Wind*, and the look sends Leva out of the shot and back (perhaps) to work in the supply room.

Comic timing: Leva, mouth full as usual, realises he may have gone too far with Warden

But the cynical comedy doesn't end there. While Leva may tell his 'topkick' to keep it in his pants and get back to work, Holmes, off for another night with his girlfriends and planning to miss 'Reveille', tells Warden: 'You ought to get out more'. Warden, primly arranging papers and casting sidelong glances at the framed photo of Karen on Holmes's desk, merely smiles, 'I've been considering it'. Holmes's pompous, even fatherly comments to his subordinate, that he will be 'leaving it in your hands', provoke 'It'll be here when you get back – Sir'.

Karen and Warden's two key romantic scenes occur in water. In the first, where Warden and Karen become lovers, it's a wet Thursday afternoon and Warden arrives slick with rain. Karen, in shorts and a striped blouse, cigarette in mouth, hesitates for a moment before letting him in. Her comments: 'better come inside before you get wet', and his smiling rejoinder, 'I am wet', would unnerve anyone not entirely certain of starting a sexual relationship. Karen knows the rules of the game and the proverbial 'score', but in her curt refusal to pour Warden's drink or to invite him to sit down (she instead surveys him from the other side of the kitchen table), she indicates her weariness and even hostility to this sort of game. Adultery and bed-hopping have always been rife in the armed forces, particularly in a peacetime army, and even if Warden is risking his career by making a pass at an officer's wife, Karen is also practised in the art. Instead of sleeping with other officers (which might end up helping her husband's career), she's had affairs with lots of enlisted men, perhaps as a way of adding class insult to marital injury. Karen admits that the thing which attracts her most to Warden – his confidence – also repels her. Warden's reply, that he 'hates to see a lovely woman going all to waste', does not bring them any closer. His 'honest' sexual desire conflicts with her equally honest sense of emptiness and self-disgust, with a ruined marriage, no job, no apparent female friends and no children. She knows he's not interested in the other sides of her life, and kisses him in a moment of self-confessed ambivalence ('I don't know, Sergeant. I just don't know'). As they kiss, Guffey pulls back out of the close-up through the kitchen window wet with rain, a neat

At opposite ends of the table: Karen, refusing to be manipulated, tears up the documents that Warden has brought along as a ploy to meet her alone; after a hostile beginning, the affair begins

bit of camerawork. It's a conventional kiss, perhaps, but hardly a conventional romantic pairing.

With Warden and Karen embarking on their affair, the scene dissolves to Maggio and Prewitt on payday. Maggio is nearly bouncing off the walls in his eagerness to leave the base and head into town to drink and screw on Hotel Street (the centre of the prewar and wartime Hawaiian red-light district was pointedly renamed 'River Street' for the film), but Prewitt, like Karen, has shut down, and lies on his bed, exhausted from a week of 'the treatment'. The camera follows the lively Maggio in his efforts to cheer Prewitt up, and at one point, he articulates the first of a number of comments in the film about the soldier's low status on the economic and social hierarchy in Hawaii. Once out of their uniforms and in the ubiquitous slacks and Hawaiian shirts 'we're as good as the rest of the world, ain't we?' White Haole girls were socially off-limits to soldiers, and even mixed-race or Japanese women were discouraged from forming relationships with enlisted men, who were known to have no money and few social prospects. Of course, if they had money to pay, soldiers could always hire a prostitute.[72] And this is where Maggio intends to take Prewitt. Only Maggio's comic effort to translate 'girls' to Prewitt (more loaded now given Clift's revealed bisexuality) gets him moving. Maggio even tosses one of his loud Hawaiian shirts over to his friend; his sister 'always buys them too big' for the scrawny Maggio.

Outside, Maylon Stark (George Reeves) notes Warden's fancy civvies, and gently warns him about Karen's well-known tendency to sleep around. When Warden brushes off the history with a smile, Stark reveals he was one of her men at a previous posting at Fort Bliss. Originally, before Cohn's urge to have a film under 120 minutes took over post-production, Taradash's scripts had a much more prominent role for Reeves (the future Superman), consisting of a drunken fight between him and Warden over Karen and a place in Maggio's death scene. Warden seems to take it lightly, and heads off for his date. The shot dissolves to a reaction shot of Karen, who's been waiting on the promenade for Warden. She is still uncertain about continuing with the affair and plays a mixture of 'Lady Astor's horse' (a glancing reference to Kerr's uptight Brit origins) and shy first date. Warden, who has stopped for a few drinks with his buddies before meeting her, is bewildered by her erratic remarks, but finally wins her over and they head off to the beach, bathing suits under their clothes. We later discover that Warden is bothered by Stark's comments and is jealous, but he conceals his feelings temporarily under a mask of resilient geniality.

Over the course of the evening, the film crosscuts between Karen and Warden's tryst at the beach and Prewitt and Maggio's evening out, where Prewitt will meet 'the Princess' prostitute Lorene and Maggio will take up with long-legged, Bette Davis-eyed Sandra (Joan Shawlee) who 'drinks like a fish'. Maggio and Prewitt stroll companionably through the famous red-light district in Honolulu; Chinese, Japanese, Hawaiian and Haole men and women throng the streets. Prewitt has a chance to be picked up by a tall, Eurasian prostitute, but Maggio drags him along to the New Congress Club, where Maggio is a card-carrying member (a subtle joke, given that the anticommunist witch hunts were still active in Hollywood). Though the PCA fought hard to make it look 'like a legitimate business enterprise', this is no dance hall.

In Jones's novel, the soldiers had regularly had 'shack jobs' with local island women, visited prostitutes and even, in Prewitt, Maggio and Sergeant Bloom's cases, gone out with wealthy gay men for drinks (and other things). Although many of the novel's references to gay relationships and subcultures were eliminated or disguised in the script (Prewitt's former bugler topkick had replaced Prewitt as the First Bugler with a current gay lover and Maggio's consorting with gay men was replaced by his implied rape by Sergeant Judson), the scenes of heterosexual sex on sale in Hotel Street were only barely concealed.[73] When he was writing his first draft script, Taradash had gone to the added trouble of changing the name of Mrs Kipfer's (Barbara Morrison) whorehouse to a 'gentleman's club' in order to

get around Geoffrey Shurlock and the PCA, but letters were still exchanged regarding whether the 'girls' were projected as 'prostitutes' or 'B-girls'. Cohn's attitude to the Code officials was simple: ' "Fuck 'em" '. As Taradash stated: 'Cohn, Adler, Zinnemann, and I all felt we would do anything to get this picture made properly'.[74]

In the end, everyone who had read the book recognised the whorehouse for what it was in the film. Mrs Kipfer, a large, richly dressed matron in black lace with an enormous bust, diamonds and marcelled curls, talks to her 'dear' Maggio in the classic faked British accent of the Edwardian madam. Zinnemann's notes directed Sinatra to repay her the compliment by inspecting her well-upholstered posterior and raising his palm to slap it, before quickly changing his mind to swing drunkenly after the younger women. A slightly drunk Prewitt leans against the front desk, as a wised-up, bleach-blonde hostess reels off the perks of Prewitt's two-dollar initiation fee at the New Congress Club. As Taradash remembered, 'Two dollars was the

Prewitt is momentarily distracted by a Eurasian prostitute but Maggio pushes him toward the New Congress Club

going rate for a cheap prostitute in those days. That's why I made it two dollars.'[75] Bleached-blonde Georgette (Kristine Miller), doll-faced and tough (she calls Prewitt 'baby face' as an uninitiated member) collects his four dollars. Clift's delivery of the line: 'What do I get for it?' left few people in any doubt of what the exchange involved. But basically, the PCA did not interfere in potentially the most controversial film since *Gone with the Wind* (where shots of childbirth, women's necklines and Rhett Butler's uttered 'damn' had exercised Shurlock's predecessor Joseph Breen). Even when they did ask for changes, such as when Lorene promises Prewitt his own key to her house and later when she says their affair is 'better' than being married, Taradash laughed: 'they were very *much* against that line, but it's in the picture … . We just ignored them'.[76] This picture of a lax 1950s code is quite different from the picture popular histories of Hollywood censorship like to present of officious prigs with overactive scissors.

Maggio prepares to slap Mrs Kipfer's (Barbara Morrison) ample behind

Set designer Frank Tuttle and art director Cary Odell added to the sense of the 'club' as a whorehouse; a tinny piano is even being played in the background, though the player hasn't learned yet 'not to hammer on the keys'. Presumably Sergeant Judson's sexual techniques would be as ham-handed as his playing, but in this scene he's not paying any attention to the girls, in contrast to the more romantic Italian-American Maggio, who puts a nickel in the juke-box, grabs the yawning Sandra, and pulls her around the dance floor in an exaggerated romantic Hawaiian dance. Later on, when Cohn was giving Zinnemann and editor William Lyon grief for not slashing the narrative to the bone, Zinnemann responded,

I think it is imperative to show a cut establishing the juke-box, because otherwise we will not know where the orchestra music comes from. This would give us the impression of a ballroom, which would be very confusing, and would establish a feeling of a dance hall rather than a whorehouse.[77]

Fatso Judson's (Ernest Borgnine) piano pounding provokes the first of several fights between him and Maggio (with Joan Shawlee as Sandra)

Judson's playing turns Maggio's glide into a jumpy jitterbug. But Prewitt isn't watching his friend's comic romantic encounter; he's already caught sight of Lorene. 'The Princess' isn't liked too much by the other working girls in the place; their stony stares in Lorene's direction contrast with Prewitt's almost open-mouthed admiration. Initially Prewitt sees Lorene sitting on a dais above the other girls in a drop-dead gorgeous Jean Louis fringed, black gown, and her simple elegance and French-sounding name (which we later learn Mrs Kipfer picked out of a perfume ad) don't seem to fit with the gum-chewing girls and the bargain basement surroundings.

Though Lorene would earn Donna Reed her only Oscar, she was no one's first choice for the role, including Fred Zinnemann. Zinnemann had hoped to cast Julie Harris, who had starred in his most recent film, *The Member of the Wedding*, but Cohn found the idea of the tawny, scrawny Harris as a Hotel Street whore unpleasant and told him to find someone else. Zinnemann and Reed had known

A low-angle shot of 'the Princess', Lorene (Donna Reed) as she looks at Prewitt for the first time

each other for over ten years and worked well together. Reed was growing tired of her good-girl roles,[78] and relished the change. Her commitment to the role soon wiped any initial doubts he had about casting her. Zinnemann's off-camera shots with Reed show them close together, almost eye to eye, her fingertips touching his wrist. Zinnemann's rapport with actors was legendary – he got close to them but never told them exactly what to do – but his relationship with Reed was complicated. His shooting script notes for Lorene indicate that she 'should have no class, no humor, no brains, great charm, tenderness and bitterness', and Reed projected her own version of Lorene, which had more than a touch of steeliness.

Reed was very upfront about her role as a prostitute, not a dance-hall girl, and gave several interviews about the finer points involved in playing Lorene. Film publicity in the press book emphasised Lorene's commodified sexuality ('Sure I'm nice to you. We're nice to all the boys'), and in a *New York Post* interview with Archer Winsten, the actress mused on her role,

How would I have made all that money in two years, enough to buy a house back home, join the country club, become respectable. I couldn't make that much just being a dance hostess. No, I suppose it wouldn't make much sense unless you were a prostitute.[79]

Hollywood columnists, old hands at comparing actresses' roles and private lives, were a bit baffled by Reed, labelling her 'Hollywood's prettiest paradox'.[80]

Shortly after playing a Honolulu prostitute, she starred as one of the great heroines of American history: Sacajawea, in *The Far Horizons* (1954), and actively campaigned for the Native American's election into the Hall of Fame. But Reed left films for tamer television roles. Later in life, known as the great American matron of *The Donna Reed Show* (ABC, 1958–66), she remarked, 'I'd love to play another bad girl if I had the time'.[81] But she would comment on the film industry's double standard for women: 'Ours is a business that's very businesslike where actors are concerned, but not where actresses are concerned. They're supposed to live in some sort of never-never land of glamor and intrigue'.[82] Lorene's blend of middle-class banality and provocativeness gave her one of the few nuanced roles of her career.

Eventually Prewitt is pulled away from his first intimate talk with Lorene to prevent his friend from attacking 'Fatso' Judson. Maggio may be small, but it takes several people to hold him off the burly, buzz-cut Fatso.[83] The latter is not only a crude bully; he's a racist, calling Maggio a 'little wop' (as we and Sinatra look up at his towering bulk). Sinatra delivers his classic, over-the-shoulder line as he gets dragged away: 'Only my friends call me wop', but Sandra consoles him by agreeing to head off to a phone booth where he will 'unveil a fifth of whisky' and presumably something else to impress her. But protecting his friend has lost Prewitt his girl; Lorene is not in the game of professional monogamy any more than Karen (but at least Lorene gets paid for her trouble). Prewitt reacts with jealousy, breaking in on the two-shot between her and a more upscale surfer soldier who's taken his place on the wickerwork settee.

The film cuts to Warden and Karen clambering over rocks to get to the secluded Halona Cove Beach outside Honolulu (shot Friday and Saturday, 24–5 April 1953). They strip down and Kerr does have a dark one-piece bathing suit under her peasant skirt. They don't exchange a word, merely challenging each other playfully with their eyes, before Karen runs off into the surf, quickly followed by Warden. Kerr recalled that their famous kiss in the surf took a whole day of rehearsals and multiple takes 'waiting for the right wave' (Code officials tried to shorten the length of the shot of them kissing in the surf). Post-kiss, Karen reveals how much of her tough exterior developed as a result of her bad marriage. Similar things will happen to Prewitt and Lorene; after a rocky start, where Lorene's work as a prostitute and 'being nice to all the boys' conflict with Prewitt's natural infatuation and belief that 'We may look all alike but we ain't all alike', she will tell him her story about being jilted by a rich

boyfriend and he will later tell her about blinding his boxing partner, Dixie Wells. Both scenes between the couples are visually linked by the matched editing of the upward spray of the surf at Halona Cove Beach and the slowly spiralling smoke of Prewitt's cigarette (which he manages to hold still and aloft while kissing Lorene, who's on top and replaces her earring with practised dexterity – another barely veiled sexual reference).

But at the same time, these narratives are linked by their shared probing of the limits of subjectivity and empathy. Karen and Warden strip down physically (the censors suggested they wear robes over their suits but were again ignored by Zinnemann), but only Karen strips down psychologically. She dominates their romantic beach scenes in a number of ways; she goes into the water first, she's on top in their famous kiss in the surf, she's the one with a past and is not jealous of Warden's conquests. When their playful exchange about

Cast and crew wait 'for the right wave' at Halona Cove Beach (BFI)

the number of men she's kissed (and where Warden ranks) turns nasty, Karen's comments, 'I had to go and forget that you were like all the rest of them', echo Lorene and Prewitt's conversation. Warden, outmatched by Karen's words, uses physical violence to subdue her (made more visceral by their bare wet bodies), but Karen regains power in the scene by offering to give him some 'gossip' for the barracks, turning his macho theatrics into a desire for 'feminine' chitchat. She reveals in close-up how her husband's drunken infidelities led to her miscarriage and sterility. The military doctors at the base hospital 'fixed her up fine' and even took her appendix out for free. She's victimised, but Kerr's delivery is paradoxically empowering. The camera holds on her throughout her narrative, which she delivers in a clear, matter-of-fact tone barely concealing her bitterness for the man who destroyed her health (the hysterectomy in the script replaced the novel's story about contracting gonorrhea from Holmes) and the men who gossip about her extramarital affairs.

Zinnemann would note that Lorene's replacement of her earring after kissing Prewitt on Mrs Kipfer's sofa was yet another veiled sexual reference that got by the Production Code Administration

Though Warden tries to stop her speech and hides his face from her eyes, she has her say. He remains a passive listener. Zinnemann's script notes indicate that he didn't want Kerr to play Karen as 'neurotic' and that she should 'forget guilt feeling' in terms of her numerous extramarital affairs. He wrote: 'Play for change of personality from frustration, tenseness to fulfillment'.[84]

Lorene then tells her story to Prewitt. She was a working-class girl from Oregon whose rich boyfriend jilted her for a more socially acceptable girl. Prewitt isn't overly moved; when she remarks that they could 'write a book about it', he smiles, replying 'thousands of them', thereby characterising her as one of thousands of disappointed women who became whores when men 'did them wrong'. Yet he says nothing when she reveals her response to the end of the relationship: she decides to come to Hawaii on the advice of another girl she met in the upwardly mobile frontier town of Seattle. She plans to make money and return to stateside respectability with 'a stocking full of money'. This dream of middle-class status is so strong she will later reject Prewitt's proposal of marriage. In contrast to the dozens of Hollywood films that had whores with hearts-of-gold hesitate or reject serious relationships and marriage so they wouldn't damage their men (*Madame X*, 1934; *Marked Woman*; *Camille*, 1937; *Stagecoach*; *Waterloo Bridge* are among the best known), Lorene knows that marrying Prewitt will damage her social status, and even Prewitt acknowledges that he's 'a private, no-class dogface'. Officer status is the one way out of this life, but for Prewitt (and also Warden, who will need to take an officer training course in order to marry Karen without damaging his career and her social status), this advancement effectively involves the prostitution of Prewitt's principles (and Warden's hatred of the officer class).

It is a credit to Taradash and Adler (who made several important women's pictures in the late 1940s) that the women's stories remain so prominent in the final script. One Columbia script reader, after looking at Taradash's first estimating script, commented,

I have heard *From Here to Eternity* described as a man's story. I think it is going to prove to be, in the picture version at least, a woman's story also … I think that the women of the movie audience are going to understand Karen and Alma [Lorene], and sympathise with them deeply.[85]

Zinnemann also emphasised the importance of their narratives, and – a rare thing for him – refused to cut Karen's and Lorene's rather lengthy dialogue in the script.

While the two romances temporarily offer the four protagonists some happiness, Zinnemann wrote,

I believe it is very important not to play either one of the love stories as an idyllic romance at any time. There must always be a sense of constraint in the scenes. A constraint imposed by the outside world, the same as it is in the book.[86]

Maggio's interruption of Lorene and Prewitt's conversation provides the only comic relief in the evening's series of depressing personal revelations. Here Sinatra's gift for graceful ad-libbing and throwaway humour give him a kind of Chaplinesque quality. He knocks, but at first only his arm bearing a pint of whisky comes through the door; then his face pops around the corner. Maggio's grin transforms any room; within seconds, Lorene and Prew are grinning away at him as much as at each other. Like the Tramp, Maggio identifies and hates the establishment's system that exploits poor enlistees such as Prewitt and ex-Gimble's basement department store clerks like himself; he recognises it on the streets of New York or in Schofield Barracks. Alcohol is a prop; he tosses the contents of a half-full glass out the window with 'Hope there's a cop under that' before pouring his 'paisan' a large drink (which he then proceeds to drink, handing the smaller one to Prewitt). The moment he exits, leaving Prewitt the bottle in an act of supreme kindness ('You need this more than I do; tomorrow you'll be back with the treatment'), their smiles fade and Prewitt's sad story takes over. Prewitt explains to Lorene that he gave

up fighting when he accidentally blinded his own friend in a boxing match. Lorene listens, obviously concerned, but says nothing as she watches him cry (something Gary Cooper would also dare to do in Zinnemann's *High Noon*), knowing all too well how useless words are. Her understanding is in contrast to Prewitt, who, earlier, had made light of her romantic disappointment.

The film dissolves to the following Monday morning, where Buckley, after carefully checking to see he isn't observed, tells Prewitt that Holmes has ordered his boxer non-coms to push 'the treatment': 'no-holds barred: they aim to run you right into the stockade if they have to'. Buoyed by his night with Lorene, Prewitt replies jauntily, 'Let 'em'. But after getting kicked in the face with mud and having to dig a five-foot trench to bury a newspaper, Prewitt is visibly exhausted that evening. His hand trembles as he drags on his cigarette and listens to Buckley, Mazzioli, Friday (Don Dubbins), and others sing the 'Re-Enlistment Blues' on their bunks. Another scene

The Chaplinesque clown: Maggio's head only emerges around the door after he waves a pint of whisky at Lorene and Prewitt

shows Prewitt scrubbing the gym floor on work detail as Holmes, in the ring, whispers to Galovitch to kick pails of bloody water over on him. Prewitt finally snaps, telling Galovitch to 'clean it up yourself' and tells Holmes that his non-commissioned officer is out of line and owes *him* an apology. Holmes responds by ordering Corporal Paluso (John L. Cason) to escort Prewitt in full field dress and pack up to the top of Kohle-Kohle pass and back – twice – without result.

Cutting to the company commander's office, Warden deftly persuades Holmes not to court-martial Prewitt but to double up on company punishment (which Warden will oversee). When Mazzioli admiringly comments 'Nice going, Sarg', Warden bawls him out, refusing to be seen as a soft touch. But in this scene Warden has made the decision to involve himself in Prewitt's stubborn revolt against Holmes and the system. Warden is off on the margins of the frame as Prewitt faces Holmes for his second hike up the mountain, but he misses nothing; Prewitt's sweat-soaked exhaustion and continued resistance and Holmes's almost fascist abuse of power: 'You can't be reasonable with a man like that; you have to treat him like an animal'. Warden's ace, that company punishment will break Prewitt, is actually Warden's way of protecting Prewitt from the stockade.

Prewitt's next scene shows him sharing a work detail with Maggio (presumably arranged by Warden). The latter, in white waiter's coat, is serving the men breakfast with his usual enthusiasm and boasts to Stark he's 'putting in for corporal tomorrow'. Stark knows 'this man's army' will never promote Maggio. Warden strolls in as Maggio goes out, laden with a huge tray. Despite his shark-like grin and mocking comments about Prewitt being 'drawn to a fine edge', Warden is actually taking an interest in Prewitt. Prewitt at first sees this as mere good-cop/bad-cop. Prewitt's eyes are shining with indignation as he faces the Sergeant over the steaming dishes. 'If you think you can bribe me into boxing Warden, you're wrong. You're wrong. Not you and Dynamite Holmes and the treatment.' Warden, smiling as ever, gently puts his coffee cup in Prewitt's sink and departs. Old-timer Pete Karelsen (Tim Ryan), who saw action with

Warden in the Philippines, knows that Warden likes Prewitt and is
keeping him on extra duty as a form of protection. They exchange
friendly insults until Warden offers to buy him a beer at Choy's.

In Choy's that night, Harry Warren and Mack Gordon's 1941
song, 'The Chattanooga Choo Choo' (made famous in Fox's *Sun
Valley Serenade*, 1941), is blaring on the juke-box as the Chinese
barman loads a tray for the elegant Polynesian waitress Rose, who,
ignoring the chorus of male wolf whistles aimed at her bottom, sways
over to Warden's table. She gets this every day and knows how to
deflect it. She smiles at Warden when he tips her extra and comes
back as he calls her softly by her name. 'Do you know why I like to
have you serve me beer?' She shakes her head ever so slightly,
intrigued. 'So's I can watch you when you walk away.' Warden gets
away with it, with Karelsen guffawing next to him. The camera cuts
to another part of the bar, where Mazzioli is advising Prewitt to lodge
a complaint against Holmes. Prewitt refuses: 'I won't give them that

Rose observed by Warden and Pete Karelsen (Tim Ryan)

satisfaction'. He does show irritation at Friday's inept bugling, however, and snatches the instrument, finally giving the company proof of why he was First Bugler, and still is, regardless of rank. Warden and Karelsen watch in the background in drunken fascination. As Taradash revealed, though Clift 'couldn't box' and had a double, 'he did learn to bugle'.[87] The room breaks out in a round of applause, which ends, ironically, with the arrival of Fatso. This scene only exists because of Harry Cohn. Several years later, Taradash spoke at Cohn's funeral and revealed,

When I first discussed *From Here to Eternity* with him I had a bead on the notion of Prew blowing Taps after Maggio's death, this to be the only time Prew would play the instrument in the film. He insisted this was wrong. He could not fortify his argument but he had a feeling that somewhere, somehow, the audience should hear that bugle played once before the climax. I disagreed violently … . But his notion stuck. It irritated. And because it did, I

As Maggio smiles, Prewitt proves to the men drinking at Choy's why he will always be First Bugler (Clift dubbed by Manny Klein)

came to the idea of the moment in the Chinese hashhouse scene when Prew, to vent his fury at the way the army is mistreating him, snatches the bugle from an inept musician and blows a wild, tortured obligato.[88]

But the scene also proved useful in developing Fatso Judson's feud with Maggio. Spotting Maggio instantly as he enters the bar, he snatches a family photo from the table. 'Who's the broad?' he asks, and then, after Maggio grudgingly admits it's his sister, Fatso kisses her portrait, whispering something foul in Prewitt's ear with a laugh. Prewitt gets up slowly, with the intention of grabbing Fatso, but Maggio, who's overheard, is too quick and slams a chair on Fatso's head. The camera moves with him and holds. The room jolts to a halt; no one moves or speaks for a moment. Fatso draws a knife, bragging he will 'cut this wop's heart out' and Warden leaps up, pushing between them. But only when Warden smashes the top off a beer bottle does the scene cut to a medium close-up of him brandishing its jagged edges. It's a riveting scene, and Zinnemann and Adler kept the broken bottle in defiance of Production Code advice (it was banned on Australian screens). When Taradash, who was watching the shooting, saw Lancaster smash the top of his beer bottle and turned anxiously to Adler, the censors on his mind, Adler replied: '"Fuck 'em"'.[89] Fatso won't go after Warden, and Lancaster's grin is terrifying as he taunts, 'Come on, Fatso, if it's killing you want, come on'. Sinatra watches as Fatso backs down, and, though still contemptuous of Fatso's threat ('Guys like you wind up in the stockade sooner or later. One day you'll walk in there I'll be waiting. I'll show you a coupla things'), he's visibly shaken.

Warden takes his cigarette outside and Prewitt, having picked up Fatso's knife, follows him out, having acknowledged to Maggio that 'he's a good man'. Warden is calmly smoking in the dark. Unlike the others who may be younger recruits, he's seen action and has taken a long time to become a professional killer. The peacetime army life is not what he likes; the fight with Fatso is about as exciting as it gets. But Prewitt is young and Warden, seeing his admiration,

grins, telling him to keep the knife for a souvenir as if he were a kid at the circus. Held in a companionable two-shot, Warden tells him he'll get a weekend pass since Holmes 'signs anything I put in front of him'.

The dissolve becomes a cloud of talcum powder. Maggio is tossing it all over him as he shouts a few bars of last night's 'The Chattanooga Choo Choo'. But his preening gets him nowhere. Prewitt, impatient to be with Lorene, leaves to catch the bus to town, and one of the sergeants puts Maggio on guard duty. Things don't go any better for Prewitt; Lorene is busy with a crowd of men from Hickham Field and has no time for him. Angry with his long absence and inability to understand her job, she sneers, 'I work here, can't you understand … . You're not my husband, you know.' But Prewitt's determination to treat her like his temperamental girlfriend and not a whore or a dance hostess, forces the confession from her: Lorene is not her real name, however beautiful he may find it. It's Alma Burke.

Warden's broken beer bottle weapon made it past the Hollywood censors, but was banned from Australian screens

'Alma?' Prewitt almost squeaks in surprise. Taradash had originally intended that she tell Prewitt her real name on the beach, almost casually, but Zinnemann rejected it, calling it a 'nothing' scene.[90] Taradash rewrote it, and the scene maintains the film's tension, even as Lorene strips off her professional veneer.

She agrees to meet him later at the small Kalakaua Inn with its multiracial clientele. So, unfortunately, does Maggio, who reels in, transforming the room and drawing all the smiles at the bar. Hungry for 'a nail' (cigarette), he trades a few quips with Prewitt and Lorene before taking the camera with him to the middle of a crowded bar. He raps on the bar for a drink and while waiting, shoots a mock game of craps with a pair of olives, calling himself 'The terror of Gimble's basement', where he used to work as a lowly packing clerk. 'Snake eyes', he slurs, turning to a talking couple with mock despondency. 'Story of my life.' As usual, Lorene and Prewitt do little but laugh affectionately at their clown. Sinatra carried the connection between

Snake eyes: Maggio will gamble with anything, even olives

his own life and failing career and Maggio's fate still further off screen, when he did a publicity shot of himself doing fatigue duty with a mop in one hand and a copy of *Variety* in the other. Although Prewitt warns his friend to slow down, Maggio has caught a glimpse of the Royal Hawaiian Hotel through a window. The year before, the hotel had served as one of the locations in John Wayne's anticommunist film for Warner Bros., *Big Jim McLain* (1952). Maggio, tearing out of the bar, plans to go to the hotel and meet 'a movie star', and it's tempting to imagine a nighttime brawl between John Wayne's HUAC investigator and the subversive Sinatra, a steadfast Roosevelt supporter who'd been dubbed the 'New Deal Crooner' by the right-wing US press.[91] But Maggio has also revealed that he walked off guard duty, and Prewitt gets up, horrified, in an attempt to get Maggio back on his post before the MPs get him. He leaves Lorene staring after him as he follows Maggio out into the night.

It turns out that he has to follow a trail of discarded clothing and slurred black humour. Maggio is half-asleep, half-naked, on a park bench, and tells Prewitt to give his clothes to the poor Indians because 'all they wear is G-strings'. Maggio may be drunk, but his humour is as sharp as ever. Given contemporaneous discussions by writers such as Mari Sandoz about the connections between Jewish and Native American holocausts in *Cheyenne Autumn* (1953), Maggio's suggestion that his army uniform be given to Native Americans is not unlike proposing that Jewish survivors of the Holocaust keep warm in ex-Nazi uniforms.[92] Equally, military slang referred to AWOL soldiers as 'off the reservation' and, as Maggio grows more resentful of people in power, he becomes a parody of the Hollywood Indian. As Prewitt moves about collecting his clothes, Maggio lolls about bare-chested, finally turning on his friend in irritation, 'Wassa matter with you? Can't a man get drunk? Can't a man do nothin'?' (ironically two charges the army and US government levelled at Native American men in the reservation system). When he spies a pair of advancing MPs, in the absence of a tomahawk, he jumps up and throws his shoes at them. Off screen, this scene was

responsible for a breakdown in relations between Zinnemann and Sinatra. In rehearsal, Clift and Sinatra had decided to change the script slightly by having Sinatra deliver his tirade standing (possibly making him look less comical and less drunk). Zinnemann, who thought this scene would make Maggio's gripes against the army look more persuasive, 'believed I could get away with shooting the scene as rehearsed'[93] but, as they were about to shoot, Cohn 'roared up' with some officers and pressured Zinnemann into shooting it as in the script. Sinatra evidently lost respect for Zinnemann, feeling that he had backed down in front of the bigshots. The actor evidently refused to speak with the director for years, which Zinnemann said, in one late interview, was 'chicken shit'. But standing up or sitting down, audiences are on Maggio's side. In retrospect, Zinnemann reasoned, 'I am surprised to think how many battles I did win'.[94]

The next scene opens on Prewitt's worried profile, as he silently waits for news of Maggio's court-martial. Warden delivers

A Hollywood Indian off the reservation. Maggio's AWOL attack on the military police will get him six months in the stockade the result with reluctance: six months, and the camera holds on Prewitt, the melancholy 'Re-Enlistment Blues' playing over the scene (in the novel, this had been a kind of work-in-progress of Friday and Prewitt). But Prewitt, 'heartsick' according to the script, knows that it's far worse than that for Maggio. Although famously we do not see Fatso beating Maggio to death, his first meeting with the Stockade Sergeant of the Guard is terrifying in its implication of brutality and implied sexual violence. In fact, many people would remember the stockade scenes as being in the film thanks to the way the writer and director handled the material. Taradash scripted it in an extremely suggestive way and Zinnemann didn't change a thing, although censors would remove Fatso's sexualised comments about Maggio ('Hard sister'). Fatso's billy club, pointed at Maggio from behind his desk, is compounded by Judson rising in his chair and Maggio's silent terror as he looks at Judson raising the club.

Although the military remarked on the 'concentration camp' aspects of the stockade sequences, Maggio's abuse by Judson had a sexual dimension in the script, music and shot composition

Maggio's incarceration initiates the second series of intercut romantic scenes but, unlike in the first set, sexual fulfilment does not bring happiness. Lorene plays a good game of house for Prewitt; she's rented a place in the 'fashionable district' on the heights above town and tells him she's had a key made for him. She tries to take his mind off Maggio; she introduces her friend Georgette as 'great' for Maggio when he gets out of the stockade. She plans out their evening, with her cooking dinner, but when Prewitt remarks that 'It's just like being married', she responds, a bit cynically, 'It's better'. This should be a cue for Prewitt to get worried.

Things seem to be going well for Karen and Warden, who are next seen out for a quiet dinner on the other side of the island. One wonders how the Production Code missed commenting on this 'other love scene where Karen bites Warden's thumb', for we're left in little doubt as to how she'd rather be spending her evening.[95] The sound of drunken laughter is heard over a close-up of Warden holding her, and

Script notes mention Karen's explicit thumb biting, but this scene also made it past censors

his face stiffens. A point-of-view shot shows officers and their dates arriving at the outdoor nightspot, and the couple gets up carefully using the trees as a screen. Warden drives her convertible back into town, its top now up, and he pulls over opposite the golf course where in a few weeks Prewitt will be shot by his own men. As Warden lights his cigarette, Karen puffs at hers in frustration, noting that even on the other side of the island they 'had to run out like jailbirds'. Warden then makes an interesting remark. Although he reasons that Holmes might let her get a divorce, 'he would never let me transfer out of his company', giving an example of how little women are valued in the military. Karen's plan to make Warden an officer offends him, but eventually, with some snarls, he agrees, and she says bitterly into his shoulder, 'And so they were married and lived unhappily ever after', perhaps the most cynical comment on Hollywood's classic romantic storyline ever. As Zinnemann mused in his production notes, 'They are lonely when they are separated, yet somehow when they are together they should seem even more lonely'.[96]

Like Karen, Prewitt has domestic plans that involve promotion, but Lorene is not as amenable as Warden. Even when she gently tells Prewitt to stop necking so they can finish dinner, he's happy and confident enough to ask her to marry him. But of course she refuses – even after he says he'll capitulate to Holmes's boxers in order to win a promotion, enabling him to provide her with a more suitable standard of living. Lorene is as driven in her way as Warden is in his. These two are the real survivors of *From Here to Eternity*; Prewitt, Maggio and Karen are the victims (though it is not certain whether Karen will divorce Holmes and restart her life after Pearl Harbor). Though Prewitt will make the first move in Mrs Kipfer's establishment, Lorene is the one to suggest the private parlour and takes the initiative in their lovemaking (like Karen in the beach kiss, Lorene is on top). When she (in close-up) describes her plans to become a proper country-club woman who buys a house for her mother back home, Lorene is relentless in her determination to erase

her past. With Zinnemann's coaching, Donna Reed gave a chilling, unsmiling delivery, which contrasts sharply with Taradash's 'impassioned' script direction.[97] Looking at Reed in these scenes, critic Manny Farber found her 'an interesting actress whenever cameraman Burnett Guffey uses a hard light on her somewhat bitter features'.[98] Prewitt, impressed but defeated, remarks that she's 'got guts'. But Lorene also envisions a life where she will be the main breadwinner and provide for her mother (without a man), before becoming 'a proper wife who can run a proper home and raise proper children. And I'll be happy because when you're proper you're safe.' She will achieve this through the erasure of her history, just like a classic Western prostitute enjoying the perks of the frontier, where American values are remade over and over again. Warden similarly cuts Karen out of his life before Pearl Harbor; even when they meet for the last time on the promenade, he's distracted by a man he mistakes for the AWOL Prewitt. Lorene has the advantage over the

Reed's chilling performance as she plans her transition from the New Congress Club to the country club

other protagonists in that she can not only talk about her past but also re-picture her future. Yet her portrait of the proper life is pointedly undercut by the ensuing sequence where a smiling Karen announces her determination to divorce her husband. So much for 'proper' marriages.

Prewitt may tell Lorene he will fight to become a sergeant and marry her, but the next day, while on fatigue duty with Private Nair, he fights publicly for the first time since he injured Dixie Wells. Nair has been in the stockade and talks about Fatso's brutal and secret beatings of Maggio and hints that soon, Maggio will 'crack' and escape. Galovitch interrupts them and Prewitt, enraged and worried about his friend, finally snaps. A crowd quickly gathers around them and, after taking a few bad punches because he worries about blinding Galovitch, he finally lets loose and knocks him out in a series of rapid cuts and close-ups (some of the sequences were filmed with Clift's stunt double). Holmes watches for some time with approval but intervenes only when he sees Galovitch losing. He intends to throw Prewitt in the stockade, but the company boxers prevent it, rallying to Prewitt's defence in a rare moment of solidarity. Though Prewitt declares that he still won't box for them, the events have another purpose. General Slater has observed Holmes's unconscionable behaviour and begins an investigation into his treatment of Prewitt. Holmes will eventually be forced to resign (behind closed doors), but it will be too late for Prewitt. By then, he will already be on the run from killing Sergeant Judson.

That night Prewitt gets drunk with his friends, and sits outside Choy's playing a version of the 'Re-Enlistment Blues' on his mouthpiece with Friday. Warden reels out of the bar with a paper-bagged bottle in hand and sings the chorus. He sits fatalistically in the middle of the road, parodying guard duty as Prewitt sees him on his way back for more beer. 'On your knees, scrub the floor!' Warden teases. Warden invites him to sit down and share the bottle, and sympathises, 'Too bad they gotta get you sooner or later. Life's crummy.' He continues to speculate: 'What do you suppose would happen if a truck was to come along here and run us over?' They start to argue drunkenly about staying together or moving, and Warden tells Prewitt about his girl 'who wants me to become … an officer'. He's disgusted with himself and worries that he might turn out to be a guy like Holmes. When Prewitt replies simply, 'a man should be what he can become', Warden strokes Prewitt's hair affectionately and reminisces about Lorene's 'beautiful name'. Lancaster played the drunk, but Clift was drunk for most of this scene, later writing a letter of apology to Zinnemann when he flubbed his lines: 'Dear Fred: The Sarge and I finished yr bottle – two measly drinks. Jesus man – how can I be a fuck-up on just one measly drink? Goodnight sir M.'[99]

At that point, Leva nearly runs them over in a jeep and, as he curses them, Maggio reels out of the bushes – nearly dead, clothes ragged, cut and bruised – and leans against the jeep. In the shooting script, Zinnemann wrote that Maggio is 'a nightmare figure, an apparition'. Prewitt grabs him, holding him in his arms as he falls to the ground. He dies in Prewitt's arms, telling him of his escape and Fatso's brutal beatings.

He whacks me in the gut and asks me if it hurts. I spit at him, like always. Only yesterday, it was bad. He hit me, he hit me, he hit me. I had to get out, Prew, I had to get out.

At last, losing breath, Maggio frets that they will take Prewitt to the stockade and kill him too. His last words are for Prew. 'Just lay there and be quiet, Prew.' He dies in Prewitt's arms and there is silence. Warden looks at his eyes. 'He's dead.' Sinatra's death scene may have won him the Oscar, but it was the last of many riveting moments in one of the best supporting performances in any Hollywood film.

Maggio's death is followed by Prewitt's playing of 'Taps', the first time he ever plays it at Schofield, and the last. He's crying and, though Zinnemann had famously asked Gary Cooper to cry in *High*

Maggio after several weeks with Judson's 'treatment'; Sinatra's performance as the doomed Maggio remains his definitive screen role

*Noon*, the director and writer Daniel Taradash had been against Prewitt crying in this scene and had fought Cohn. This was one of the few battles that Cohn won. The final song is played across a series of close-ups of the men in the barracks, and then gradually, growing groups of men coming outside to watch Prewitt in the night. They don't talk, they just listen, but their loneliness is made more poignant for audiences who know that within a couple of weeks, many of these men will be dead. Maggio's death also initiates Prewitt's death. From the moment Maggio dies, Prewitt ceases to care about himself at all and walks past Warden without a word. The scene dissolves to the exterior of the New Congress Club where Prewitt is waiting for Fatso to come out. Once the sound of the hammered piano stops, Prewitt approaches the lumbering sergeant and persuades him to come into an alley. They fight in the shadows, and Fatso falls, killed by the very knife with which he first threatened Maggio.

Shot in a striking low-angle composition, the men listen to Prewitt play 'Taps' for the last time, in memory of Maggio

Prewitt stumbles back to Lorene and Georgette, bleeding in the belly, and tumbles down the stairs. Though Warden reads headlines about 'The Killer of the Stockade Sergeant', he does nothing about it and has Sergeant Dhom cover for his absences. Warden ignores Dhom's worries about 'carrying' Prewitt, and continues to read the paper, his feet on the desk. No wonder Warden does nothing. Captain Holmes is under investigation and he is forced to resign (but he isn't court-martialled). The new company commander Captain Ross (John Bryant) tells an abashed line of sergeants that no one will earn promotions through boxing any longer and has Mazzioli remove the boxing photos on the walls. Warden seems to like Ross (his decision to bust Galovitch and put him in charge of the latrines provokes another gleaming smile), but he's temporarily discomposed when Ross takes a phone call and hands him the receiver with a smile. It's Karen, and Warden knows what she wants to meet about. Ross gracefully retires. Warden leans against the wall, the camera panning with him, and he makes a date to see her later. The calendar on the wall reads 6 December.

At Kuhio Beach Park, the two sit on the same bench in the same postures as on their first date. But Karen isn't in a bathing dress and Warden is in uniform, not a trendy sports jacket. As before, Karen says what he cannot say. Warden's failure to put in his application to become an officer has nothing to do with their current situation: 'You just don't want to marry me. You're already married – to the army.' Karen's bleak monotone echoes Lorene's grim determination to achieve social respectability in an earlier scene. Code officials had asked Adler to add something at this point to emphasise the moral wrongness of Warden and Karen's affair,[100] but Kerr's emotionally dead delivery confounded these efforts, indicating the futility of social convention in the absence of love. Karen shades her eyes from the sun, at the same time giving Warden a half-wave goodbye. Karen isn't afraid of looking at things squarely; it's Warden who is the coward. She stares at him and into the setting sun for a moment, and then turns away slowly.

As she passes a road sign, we are again reminded that Pearl Harbor isn't so far away.

While Prewitt remains drunk and AWOL with Lorene, Sunday morning's breakfast turns into a nightmare. Clocks on the wall read eight minutes to eight a.m. (clocks play occasional but pivotal roles in Zinnemann's other work, especially *High Noon* and *Day of the Jackal*, 1973). The sound of the clock tower and the hum of planes build until bombs start shaking the barracks. *From Here to Eternity* integrates Al Brick's footage of the attack with reconstructions from *December 7th* with shots of Nair getting strafed by Japanese Zero bullets and Warden and Karelsen bringing down a plane with a machine gun from the roof. Amid the scenes of dated destruction, which look like period pieces alongside Guffey's new footage, Lancaster fulfils his heroic role and brings down one of the enemy

Lancaster and Kerr rehearse Warden and Karen's last meeting with dialogue coach Jus Addiss

Al Brick's footage of the attack was also used by Gregg Toland for *December 7th* (1943); Warden delivers a rare good PR shot for the army (and brings down a lone Japanese plane)

planes for America, giving the army at least one good PR shot. Prewitt finally sobers up and Lorene, realising that she will lose him forever, says she will marry him if he agrees not to rejoin his unit. But he does, travelling silently at night in his civvies (the scene was shot on the golf course in the day using filters). The unhealed knife wound in his side opens up as he is running, and a group of soldiers mistakes him for a Japanese soldier and guns him down. As he falls face forward into a sandpit, the 'Re-Enlistment Blues' returns in a whisper. Warden comes to identify the body, his face inscrutable even in close-up, and delivers Prewitt's epitaph: 'He was a good soldier. He loved the army more than any soldier I ever knew.' He takes Prewitt's mouthpiece and leaves the men to remove the body. It's done quickly, with no lingering footage.

Not only was there now a war on screen, but off screen, Zinnemann was also fighting Cohn for as much time as possible to put the final cut together. The studio head's plans to open the film in August were putting Zinnemann through his own treatment, pushing him and William Lyon to put the cut together in a day. As the exasperated director wrote to Cohn,

Some time ago you promised me that for the first preview the film would be cut the way I had it in mind ... you know very well that we have gone to the other extreme. Under normal circumstances a director would certainly take a minimum of three to four weeks in order to cut a picture of this size and in order to bring out all the values to the best advantage. So far I have had *four hours* with the cutter. During that time I have gone over the first six reels, superficially and in great haste.[101]

The memo worked, with help from Adler, and Zinnemann got two more weeks to edit.

On the boat home, Karen is standing on deck watching the islands recede. Many of the women and children are being sent back to the states. Lorene is beside her in a two-shot, but Karen does not recognise her until Lorene begins to tell the story of being a Pearl Harbor 'widow'. Her 'fiancé' was a bomber pilot who died trying to taxi his plane. 'Maybe you read about it in the papers. He was awarded the Silver Star' and his fine southern family gave it to her. His name? Robert E. Lee Prewitt. In close-up, Karen jerks her head quickly to look at Lorene, who is staring out at the islands, twisting the trumpet mouthpiece in her fingers (presumably given to her by Warden). Karen, though troubled, says nothing. Lorene's myth, and the myth of the Good War and the tragedy of Pearl Harbor, will endure and replace the misfits and nobodies of the peacetime army and *From Here to Eternity*. Off screen, Warden will become the great heroic soldier he was born to be, and Lorene will buy her house, join the country club and become proper. As Zinnemann noted during shooting, for 'the ending make it clear that at last Lorene has set up the perfect lie for herself'.[102] Cohn was totally baffled by the irony, thinking Lorene had gone crazy. As Taradash remembered: 'She's giving this really extraordinary expression on her face, which is really

Lorene, travelling to the states on the same boat as Karen, has cleaned up her backstory, one of many people to remake the myth of Pearl Harbor

Off camera and back from the dead. Montgomery Clift breaks in on Kerr and Reed's last scenes, turning her faked pathos into another comic moment (AMPAS)

*no* expression but it works, and her readings are great, and he's saying, "The audience is gonna think she's meshugah"'.[103]

\*     \*     \*

The final image in the film is of the two leis Karen has tossed into the water. The legend, she says, is that if they float back into shore you'll come back; if they don't, you won't. America has as much chance of ever coming back to that point in 1941 as Jay Gatsby has of repeating the past and the rest of us have of escaping it. Although historians and cultural critics are now problematising the mythology of World War II and patriotic consensus, exploring the racial, class and gender inequities rife in the US, the complex relationships among men in the military and the end of American 'empire',[104] *From Here to Eternity*'s critical perspective on Americans at the dawn of Henry Luce's vaunted 'American Century' appeared decades before this other work and focused on women in a man's world in ways even Jones had not considered. And Zinnemann further pointed out that the film came out long before the Vietnam War and Watergate, at a point when Americans had not yet collectively confronted their flawed democracy and Pacific empire. The navy's response in 1953 was to ban the film and forbid any serviceman from seeing it. As one New York critic drily responded: 'Americans have a monumental capacity for kidding themselves … . They would like to think that their fighting men content themselves exclusively with recreation of the table-tennis and Coke voltage'.[105] *Los Angeles Times* critic Edwin Schallert admired the film, but acknowledged that it was 'subversive' and 'goes all-out in making the military situation look its worst, and could probably be used by alien interests for subversive purposes if they happened to want to make capital of this production'.[106] Jesse Zunser agreed:

There has been no attempt to make angels of the playful girls in the New Congress Club, to blunt the amorality of the seductive wife of Company G's commanding officer or hide his own amorous escapades away from home; or to soften the book's bitter indictment of the army's occasional brass-hat brutality and the enlisted man's helplessness against unofficially condoned khaki cruelty and sadism.[107]

Although Zinnemann had been worried that, as with *High Noon*, his foreign, Jewish background would provoke criticism, ironically only the *Nation*'s Manny Farber took shots at his 'unAmerican' background, writing that the film 'often makes you wish its director, Zinnemann, knew as much about American life as he does about the art of telling a story with a camera'.[108]

Most critics of the time saw it as a landmark film, 'important from any angle ... and in many instances a much better motion picture than the novel was a book' which 'will rate with the all-time greats in the ranks of motion pictures having armed forces backgrounds'.[109] British critics seemed pleasantly surprised that America could produce something so self-critical, and yet so generally popular. Though Zinnemann had been worried about ex-Nazi Germany's response to a film that critiqued its conquerors, German audiences loved *From Here to Eternity*, seeing Prewitt and Warden's dilemmas as an American equivalent of Erich Maria Remarque's anti-war classic *All Quiet on the Western Front*.[110] While all the major cast members were singled out for their outstanding work, national and international critics and audiences agreed: 'Sinatra is a revelation.'[111] The army's most vocal critic, Zinnemann's Chaplinesque clown with the courage to die for talking back, won the hearts of an audience still on the side of the underdog.

Over the years, others in film, television and theatre have tried to capitalise on the notoriety and acclaim of the 1953 film, from a six-hour television miniseries starring Natalie Wood, William Devane and Kim Basinger in 1979 (first aired, rather soppily, on Valentine's Day) to an unsuccessful thirteen-part spinoff in 1980 (which featured miniseries cast members Devane and Basinger in repeat performances) to the even less successful musical by Tim Rice (announced in May 2011 to coincide with the uncensored novel's release in e-book heavily publicised by the author's daughter Kaylie). Critics dubbed the latter *From Here to November*, and the show lasted only six months after its London opening in October 2013, despite the fact that cast members patrolled the streets in leis and Hawaiian shirts 'soliciting' for ticket sales.[112]

With every work of art and literature now a 'cultural production' with multimedia tie-ins, it's difficult to find intelligent historians or critics still willing to grapple straight-faced with concepts such as originality, complexity and integrity. But Buddy Adler may have said it in 1954: 'Something like *Eternity* happens only once in a long, long time'. For what it's worth, the American Film Institute (AFI) ranked the film number fifty-two in its poll of the best American movies ever made (1998), but it did not make any of *Sight & Sound*'s top 100 lists. That said, the AFI's genre classification doesn't really work for a genre hybrid like *From Here to Eternity* (and 'war film', for which it might just qualify, is famously omitted from the AFI's genre lists). *Sight & Sound*'s director-based ranking system may suit the collaborative production of *Eternity* even less (and *Sight & Sound*'s 'godfather' of film and film-maker rankings, Andrew Sarris, disliked Zinnemann in particular). Other critics often use *From Here to Eternity* as a way of shaming more recent Hollywood films about Pearl Harbor and World War II. For instance, A. O. Scott's tart review of *Pearl Harbor* (2001) opens with a glowing assessment of *From Here to Eternity*, the 'durable 1953 melodrama', and then dismisses the Michael Bay–Jerry Bruckheimer production by twisting Winston Churchill's comment: 'never have so many spent so much on so little'.[113] In 2003, Kenneth Turan of the *Los Angeles Times* argued that '*From Here to Eternity* remains, half a century later, a singular cinematic experience, one of the landmarks of American film'.[114] Film critic Joe Morgenstern also pointed to *From Here to Eternity* as a lesson for Hollywood's current breed of 'know-nothing' film-makers,[115] and it's regularly screened at retrospectives for stars Burt Lancaster and Frank Sinatra. Late in life, Taradash acknowledged that *From Here to Eternity*'s non-conformism was not a popular theme in 1951 or even today in motion picture terms. I don't think executives or studios are telling all the other producers, 'For God's sake, find me a story about the individual versus society'. 'Find me a great love story', they'll say. Or one with good explosions.[116]

At the time of its release, however, *From Here to Eternity* was seen as the key to regenerating more than Frank Sinatra's career. Harry Cohn's publicity campaign was unique in that it was the first time he had publicly put his name to a film from his studio.[117] Yet, unlike Jack Warner's 'theft' of producer Hal Wallis's Best Picture Oscar for *Casablanca* ten years before, Cohn had the good grace to let Buddy Adler claim the prize (admittedly Cohn was ill at the time and unable to attend the ceremonies). Columbia spent a long time exorcising the demons of its Poverty Row origins but, as other studios were losing money and cutting contracts, Cohn proved films could still do what literature, television and theatre couldn't: shoot a multimillion dollar picture in forty-one days, keep within budget and reap a huge global profit. It was an old-fashioned, production-line formula which thumbed its nose at independent productions and foreign 'art' cinema, gambled with declining audiences and won. But his health was deteriorating and only close friends, including Frank Sinatra, were allowed to visit his hospital bed. His early death in 1958 came as a shock for most of the film community. Joan Cohn asked Taradash to be an honorary pallbearer and, at the service, the writer remembered Columbia's legendary studio head primarily for hating bullshit and fancy costume pictures: 'Promise me', he said once to Taradash, 'you'll never write a picture where the characters walk out of a room backwards.'[118] Taradash believed that Cohn 'lived more minutes to the hour than anyone I ever met'.[119] But Hollywood was dealt an even harder blow with the death of Buddy Adler in 1960.

In the 1950s, Hollywood insiders would see Adler as 'the most successful example of the new generation of movie mogul, a group that may or may not save the industry from threatened extinction'.[120]

The threat was very real, with declining box office from television, deaccession of theatre holdings and the slow breakup of the studio system through independent production, union difficulties and anticommunist purges. Critics were beginning to call the box-office patron 'the new vanishing American'.[121] Enter Adler, in many ways Hollywood's ultimate Prince Charming producer (nicknamed 'The Silver Fox'), right down to the thick grey hair, chiselled features and slim six-foot build. He was even married to beautiful blonde star, Anita Louise (*A Midsummer Night's Dream*, 1935). Not only could he cope with Cohn's attempts to interfere with the script and production and the military brass's efforts to blunt *From Here to Eternity*'s critical edge, but he could produce a standard ratio, black-and-white historical film in the year of CinemaScope, 3-D and television, which made millions for the studio.[122] Adler recognised early on that 'the war marked the definite ascendancy of pictures with a subject over pictures with only a theme'.[123] The taste for realism, which he and other Hollywood film-makers believed they found during the war by working with the armed forces on documentaries, was not something he wanted to let go of postwar, but as a West Coast theatre owner and exhibitor before he turned producer, he realised audience tastes had changed and showed European pictures rather than standard Hollywood fare. *From Here to Eternity* was in many senses an achievement of Adler's vision for a Hollywood 'realist' style. Six years after he picked up his Oscar for *Eternity*, he was dead from cancer at the age of fifty-one. For many, he had been a symbol of the effort to regenerate Hollywood, as Bob Thomas argued, 'a second-generation movie maker who brought the same enthusiasm to the business that the pioneers did'.[124] For twenty-five years, industry insiders had mourned MGM executive Irving Thalberg's early death and its impact on quality film-making; Adler's end in 1960, at a point when the industry was even more vulnerable, was arguably more of a tragedy.

Although Donna Reed would move away from films and become a television byword and Clift, disfigured by a car accident a few years later, was increasingly crippled by alcohol and drug addiction, Taradash, Zinnemann, Lancaster, Kerr and Sinatra defied Hollywood's metaphors of decline and fall. Taradash would become one of Hollywood's most celebrated writers in the 1950s thanks to his work on the film (he would go on to write *Picnic*, 1955; *Storm Center*, 1956; and *Bell, Book and Candle*, 1958). As he reminisced in 1959,

'In the old days a writer was kind of like a guy in uniform before Pearl Harbor ... he was afraid to go into the best hotels' ... . But now, 'Production heads are getting the idea that writers can do more than just sit at a typewriter. They are now allowed – even welcomed – on the set'.[125]

Taradash rose still higher, serving as president of the Academy from 1970–3. Zinnemann won the Directors Guild Award more than once, even took home his own Best Picture Oscar for producing *A Man for All Seasons* (1966) and remained an active international film-maker till 1982, when he released *Five Days One Summer*. Sinatra (*The Man with the Golden Arm*, 1955; *Pal Joey*, 1957; *The Manchurian Candidate*, 1962; *Von Ryan's Express*, 1965), Lancaster (*The Sweet Smell of Success*, 1957; *The Leopard*, 1963; *Atlantic City*, 1980; *Tough Guys*, 1986) and Kerr (*Beloved Infidel*, 1959, *The Night of the Iguana*; *The Gypsy Moths*, 1969) had remarkably long-lived careers, with Lancaster and Sinatra remaining in the public eye until their deaths in the 1990s.

The fact that *From Here to Eternity* remained defiantly critical, violent and erotic, and was told with the best of Hollywood's professional artistry, continues to stun American and international audiences raised on a professionalised film criticism invested in viewing Hollywood as a conservative and self-censoring 'dream factory'. Production documents and interviews with *Eternity*'s film-makers reveal instead that they refused to conform to industry and military demands for censorship just as they refused to make a typical flag-waving war film or saccharine romantic melodrama. The credit

for *Eternity* rests with Fred Zinnemann and a group of Hollywood professionals who made the film one of the most complex, poignant and unheroic portraits of ordinary people at the dawn of the American century, unequalled in or outside Hollywood. The film remains what Harry Cohn first dreamed it would be: a moneymaker and a masterpiece.

Shooting Pearl Harbor might have been easier. Zinnemann, twenty-three years after *From Here to Eternity*, at work on *Julia* (1977), with Chic Waterson (AMPAS)

# Notes

**1** 'Inside Buddy Adler', *Screen Producers Guild Journal* vol. 2 no. 12 (1954), pp. 2–4.
**2** Archer Winsten, '*From Here to Eternity* Bows at Capitol with Huge Cast, Five Starring Roles', *New York Times*, 6 August 1953.
**3** *Variety*'s figures cover only US and Canadian rentals. Since Columbia Pictures studio records no longer exist, it is impossible to gauge its foreign earnings. The film was second at the box office in 1953, outdistanced only by *The Robe*.
**4** 'Censored', *Look*, 25 August 1953; 'The Love Scene You'll Talk About', *Picturegoer*, 14 November 1953; Helen Itria, 'Burt Lancaster: The Story of a Hard Man', *Look* vol. 17 no. 21, 20 October 1953, pp. 94–5; Fred Zinnemann, *An Autobiography* (London: Bloomsbury, 1992), p. 125; 'An Oral History with Daniel Taradash' (Beverley Hills, CA: AMPAS, 2001), p. 120; Roger Ebert, '100 Great Movie Moments', *Chicago Sun-Times*, 23 April 1995.
**5** Fred Zinnemann, *An Autobiography*, p. 119; see also Fred Zinnemann quoted in Gordon Gow, 'Individualism against Machinery' [1976], in Gabriel Miller (ed.), *Fred Zinnemann Interviews* (Jackson: University Press of Mississippi, 2004), p. 59.
**6** Peter Biskind, *Seeing Is Believing: How I Learned to Stop Worrying and Love the Fifties* (London: Pluto Press, 1983); Jane Hendler, *Best-Sellers and Their Film Adaptations in Postwar America* (New York: Peter Lang, 2001), pp. 31–2; Stephen J. Whitfield, *The Culture of the Cold War* (Baltimore, MD: Johns Hopkins University Press, 1996); Rebecca Bell-Metereau, '1953: Movies and Our Secret Lives', in Murray Pomerance (ed.), *American Cinema in the 1950s: Themes and Variations* (New Brunswick, NJ: Rutgers University Press, 2005), pp. 89–110.
**7** Michael Korda, *Making the List: A Cultural History of the American Best Seller* (New York: Barnes & Noble, 2001).
**8** Burroughs Mitchell to James Jones, 29 November 1950, box 36, folder 536, Jones Papers, Beinecke Rare Book and Manuscript Library, Yale University, New Haven, CT.
**9** *New York Times*, 6 November 1951; *Variety*, occasionally known to inflate things, gave the figure as $85,000 (5 March 1951).
**10** Bob Thomas, *King Cohn: The Life and Times of Hollywood Mogul Harry Cohn* (New York: New Millennium Press, 1967), p. 303.
**11** Norman Mailer to Burroughs Mitchell, 21 December 1950, *Selected Letters of Norman Mailer*, ed. J. Michael Lennon (New York: Random House, 2014), p. 75.
**12** James Jones, *From Here to Eternity* (New York: Scribners, 1951), p. 47.
**13** Ibid., pp. 9, 17.
**14** 'Books of the Times', *New York Times*, 26 February 1951. See also '*From Here to Eternity* Banned in Three Cities', *Publisher's Weekly*, 24 March 1951.
**15** Burroughs Mitchell to James Jones, 26 April 1950, box 36, folder 538; Jones to Mitchell, December 1950, box 36, folder 537, Jones Papers.
**16** Ibid.
**17** Alison Flood, 'Censored Gay Sex Scenes in *From Here to Eternity* Revealed', *Guardian*, 13 November 2009.

**18** Ray Bell to Harry Cohn, 13 March
1951, box 28, folder 342, Jones Papers.
**19** Frank Dorn to Columbia Pictures,
31 March 1951, box 36, folder 342, Jones
Papers, and Comments and References,
Department of Defense Files, RG 33,
entry 141, box 705, National Archives,
College Park, MD.
**20** Bell to Cohn, 13 March 1951, box 28,
folder 342, Jones Papers; Report on
*From Here to Eternity*, 20 March 1951,
box 28, folder 342, Jones Papers; E. P.
Hogan, Notes on *From Here to Eternity*,
22 March 1951, box 28, folder 342,
Jones Papers.
**21** Harry Cohn to James Jones, 29 June
1951, box 34, folder 490, Jones Papers.
**22** M. A. Schmidt, 'On the Elevation of
Mr. Adler', *New York Times*, 27 September
1953, Adler clippings, AMPAS.
**23** 'An Oral History with Daniel
Taradash', p. 216.
**24** Ibid., pp. 209–10.
**25** Ibid.
**26** Ibid.
**27** Ibid., p. 211. And not just any agent:
Zinnemann's was Abe Lastfogel,
President of the William Morris
Agency.
**28** Story Conference between Kruger
and Sylvan Simon, 13 March 1951,
box 343, folder 349, Jones Papers.
**29** 'An Oral History with Daniel
Taradash', p. 194.
**30** Ibid.
**31** Ibid.
**32** Taradash, *From Here to Eternity*
Notions, box 40, folder 7, Taradash
Papers, American Heritage Center,
Laramie, WY.
**33** Ibid.

**34** Whitfield, *The Culture of the Cold War*,
p. 63.
**35** 'An Oral History with Daniel
Taradash', p. 214.
**36** Dorn to Columbia Pictures, 31 March
1951, box 28, folder 342, Jones Papers;
Comments and References, Department
of Defense Files, RG 330, entry 141, box
705, National Archives; Clair Towne,
Undated Comments on *From Here to
Eternity*, box 28, folder 342, Jones Papers.
**37** 'An Oral History with Daniel
Taradash', p. 214.
**38** Ibid., p. 217.
**39** Ned Brown (MCA) to James Jones,
17 March 1952 and Brown to Jones,
26 December 1952, box 36, folder 526,
Jones Papers.
**40** James Jones to Ned Brown, 29 April
1952, box 36, folder 526, Jones Papers.
**41** 'An Oral History with Daniel
Taradash', p. 222.
**42** Fred Zinnemann to Harry Cohn,
undated, box 28, folder 360, Fred
Zinnemann Papers, AMPAS.
**43** 'An Oral History with Daniel
Taradash', p. 222.
**44** Ibid.
**45** Fred Zinnemann, 'Notes on *From Here
to Eternity*', 30 September 1952, 10pp, 6,
box 28, folder 360, Zinnemann Papers;
ibid., white note attached to back of
notes.
**46** Ibid.
**47** Fred Zinnemann, 'Further Notes on
*From Here to Eternity*', 23 October 1952,
2pp, back page of notes; Zinnemann,
'Notes on *From Here to Eternity*', 30
September 1952, p. 9.
**48** Boyd Martin to Fred Zinnemann,
10 November 1952 and Fred Zinnemann

to Barea College President, 12 November 1952, Box 28, folder 346, Zinnemann Papers.

**49** Zinnemann, *An Autobiography*, pp. 112–23.

**50** 'An Oral History with Daniel Taradash', p. 267.

**51** Fred Zinnemann quoted in Michael Buckley, 'Fred Zinnemann: An Interview' [1983], in Miller, *Fred Zinnemann Interviews*, p. 91; Zinnemann, *An Autobiography*, pp. 121–2.

**52** Ibid.

**53** Montgomery Clift to Fred Zinnemann, undated, box 102, folder 41, Zinnemann Papers.

**54** Hedda Hopper, 'Elusive Monty Clift Is Purist about Work', *Los Angeles Times*, 9 August 1953.

**55** Zinnemann, *An Autobiography*, p. 123.

**56** Shooting schedule, production no. 1271, 15pp, Zinnemann Papers.

**57** Zinnemann, *An Autobiography*, p. 124.

**58** '*From Here to Eternity*', *Colliers*, 7 August 1953, pp. 28–9.

**59** Martin to Zinnemann, 10 November 1952 and Zinnemann to Barea College President, 12 November 1952, box 28, folder 346, Zinnemann Papers.

**60** Fred Zinnemann, Notes removed from *From Here to Eternity* Shooting Script, box 28, folder 362, AMPAS.

**61** Patricia Bosworth, *Montgomery Clift: A Biography* (New York: Limelight, 1978), p. 25.

**62** Kate Buford, *Lancaster: An American Life* (New York: Knopf, 2000), *Fred Zinnbemann Interviews*, p. 128.

**63** Ibid., p. 129.

**64** 'An Oral History with Daniel Taradash', p. 212.

**65** Zinnemann, quoted in Miller, *Fred Zinnemann Interviews*, p. 91.

**66** 'A New Role for Deborah Kerr', *Woman's Own*, 12 November 1953.

**67** 'An Oral History with Daniel Taradash', p. 271

**68** Turner's frontier thesis was first delivered in 1893, the year the US government annexed Hawaii, the future site of Schofield Barracks and the location of the Pacific fleet (Frederick Jackson Turner, 'The Significance of the Frontier in American History' [1893], in *The Frontier in American History* (New York: Henry Holt & Co., 1921), pp. 1–38).

**69** National Centre for Health Statistics, *Marriage and Divorce Statistics United States, 1867–1967*, Series 21, Number 24, December 1973, http://www.cdc.gov/nchs/data/series/sr_21/sr21_024.pdf.

**70** Susan Douglas, *Where the Girls Are: Growing Up Female with the Media* (New York: Times Books, 1995).

**71** Lt. Col. E. P. Hogan on 22 March 1951, 3pp, box 28, folder 342, Jones Papers.

**72** Beth Bailey and David Farber, *The First Strange Place: Race and Sex in World War II Hawaii* (Baltimore, MD: Johns Hopkins University Press, 1992).

**73** More recent early drafts of the novel reveal that Jones had intended a more forceful discussion of gay relationships in the military.

**74** 'An Oral History with Daniel Taradash', pp. 227, 228.

**75** Ibid., p. 219.

**76** Ibid.

**77** Zinnemann to Harry Cohn, 18 June 1953, box 27, folder 353, Zinnemann Papers.

**78** Charles Denton, 'A Good Girl Makes Good: Donna Reed', *Los Angeles Examiner, TV Weekly*, 12 March 1961.

**79** Archer Winsten, 'Reviewing Stand', *New York Post*, 2 August 1953, clipping, box 28, folder 344, Zinnemann Papers.

**80** Paramount publicity (1954), Donna Reed clippings, AMPAS.

**81** Denton, 'A Good Girl Makes Good', pp. 3, 6. Reed may have risked typecasting had she starred in Buddy Adler's *The Revolt of Mamie Stover* (1956). The story of a wartime Honolulu prostitute and real estate speculator has clear resonances with Lorene's experience in *From Here to Eternity*.

**82** Ibid.

**83** Borgnine was cast by Max Arnow, and would go on to star in the Academy Award-wining *Marty* for Burt Lancaster's production company in 1955.

**84** Notes, removed from final shooting script, box 28, folder 362, Zinnemann Papers.

**85** J. Crow, 'Notes on First Estimating Draft', annotated by Fred Zinnemann, 23 December 1952, 5pp, 2, box 28, folder 358, Zinnemann Papers.

**86** Zinnemann, 'Notes on *From Here to Eternity*', 30 September 1952, p. 4, box 28, folder 360, Zinnemann Papers.

**87** 'An Oral History with Daniel Taradash', p. 236. Clift's bugling is dubbed by Manny Klein.

**88** Daniel Taradash, 'I Remember Him Well', p. 4, box 2, folder 32, Taradash Papers.

**89** 'An Oral History with Daniel Taradash', p. 227.

**90** Ibid., p. 224.

**91** Michael Freedland, *All the Way: A Biography of Frank Sinatra* (London: Weidenfeld & Nicolson, 1997), p. 97.

**92** Mari Sandoz, *Cheyenne Autumn* (New York: McGraw-Hill Book Company, 1953). See also Suzanne Clark, *Cold Warriors: Manliness on Trial in the Rhetoric of the West* (Carbondale: Southern Illinois University Press, 2000) and Brendan C. Lindsay, *Murder State: California's Native American Genocide, 1846–1873* (Lincoln: University of Nebraska Press, 2015).

**93** Zinnemann, *An Autobiography*, pp. 130–1. Taradash's version in his oral history is incorrect, due largely to the fact that he wasn't present at the event or while the cast and crew were in Hawaii.

**94** Ibid.

**95** Zinnemann, cutting notes to use this scene, 14 May 1953, box 27, folder 353, Zinnemann Papers.

**96** Daniel Taradash, *From Here to Eternity*, 1st Estimating Script, 17 December 1952, p. 104, box 11, folder 1, Montgomery Clift Papers, T-Mss 1967-006.

**97** Zinnemann, 'Notes on *From Here to Eternity* (Odds and Ends)', 25 October 1952, 5pp, p. 4.

**98** Manny Farber, '*From Here to Eternity*', *Nation*, 29 August 1953, p. 178.

**99** Clift to Zinnemann, undated, box 27, folder 340, Zinnemann Papers.

**100** Also noted briefly by Leonard Leff and Jerold Simmons, *The Dame in the Kimono* (London: Weidenfeld & Nicholson, 1990), p. 188.

**101** Fred Zinnemann to Harry Cohn, 29 May 1953, box 27, folder 353, Zinnemann Papers.

**102** Zinnemann, 'Notes on *From Here to Eternity* (Odds and Ends)'.

**103** 'An Oral History with Daniel Taradash', p. 257. 'Meshugah' means 'crazy' in Yiddish.

**104** Bailey and Farber, *The First Strange Place*; Allan Bérubé, *Coming Out under Fire: The History of Gay Men and Women in World War II* (New York: Penguin, 1990); Emily Rosenberg, *A Date Which Will Live: Pearl Harbor in American Memory* (Durham, NC: Duke University Press, 2003).

**105** *New York World Telegram*, editorial, 3 September 1953. See also 'Navy Bans Two Films: *Moon* and *Eternity*', reprint from *Daily News Los Angeles*, 29 August 1953.

**106** Edwin Schallert, '*From Here to Eternity* Blasts Viewers with Atomic Power', *Los Angeles Times*, 1 October 1953, p. B11.

**107** Jesse Zunser, '*From Here to Eternity*', *Cue*, 8 August 1953, p. 16.

**108** Farber, '*From Here to Eternity*'.

**109** *Variety*, 29 July 1953; *Hollywood Reporter*, 29 July 1953.

**110** Gerhard Schulz-Rehden, '*Verdammt in alle Ewigkeit*', *Norddeutsche Zeitung*, 10 April 1954; MH, 'US–Barras im Scheinwerferlicht', *Hamburger Echo*, 6 February 1954, box 28, folder 342, Zinnemann Papers.

**111** *Motion Picture Daily*, 29 July 1953.

**112** A West End Whinger, 18 October 2013, http://westendwhingers. wordpress.com/2013/10/18/review-from-here-to-eternity-shaftesbury-theatre/.

**113** A. O. Scott, 'War Is Hell, But Very Pretty', *New York Times*, 25 May 2001.

**114** Kenneth Turan, '*Eternity* Is, Quite Simply, Timeless', *Los Angeles Times*, 5 December 2003.

**115** Joe Morgenstern, 'Worldly Wisdom', *Wall Street Journal*, 13 May 2006.

**116** 'An Oral History with Daniel Taradash', p. 208.

**117** Thomas, *King Cohn*, p. 310.

**118** Taradash, 'I Remember Him Well', pp. 3, 5, Taradash Papers.

**119** Ibid.

**120** Bob Thomas, 'Studio Boss Is Indeed a Buddy', Adler Clippings, AMPAS.

**121** Howard McClay, 'Buddy Adler', *Los Angeles Daily News*, 2 October 1952, Adler Clippings.

**122** 'Inside Buddy Adler', p. 2.

**123** Frank Daugherty, 'Buddy Adler, Exhibitor-Producer', *New York Times*, 16 April 1950.

**124** Bob Thomas, 'Adler Passing Mourned by All in Film Business', *Mirror-News*, 3 September 1960.

**125** Hal Boyle, 'Writer No Longer Low Man of Films, Says Taradash', *Mirror-News*, 7 January 1959.

# Credits

**From Here to Eternity**
USA/1953

**Production Company**
Columbia Pictures
Corporation
**Producer**
Buddy Adler
**Director**
Fred Zinnemann
**Assistant Director**
Earl Bellamy
**Screenwriter**
Daniel Taradash
Based upon the novel
*From Here to Eternity* by
James Jones
**Script Supervisor**
Charlsie Bryant
(uncredited)
**Director of Photography
(b/w)**
Burnett Guffey, A.S.C.
**Still Photographer**
Irving Lippman
**Assistant Cameraman**
Val O'Malley
**Editor**
William Lyon, A.C.E.
**Art Director**
Cary Odell
**Set Decorator**
Frank Tuttle
**Gowns**
Jean Louis
**Makeup**
Clay Campbell
Robert J. Schiffer
(uncredited)
**Hairstylist**
Helen Hunt

**Musical Director**
Morris Stoloff
**Music (background)**
George Duning
**Orchestrations**
Arthur Morton
**Song**
'Re-Enlistment Blues'
James Jones, Fred Karger
and Robert Wells
**Supervising Sound
Editor**
John P. Livadary
**Sound Engineer**
Lodge Cunningham
**Stunts**
John L. Cason
**Casting**
Max Arnow

**CAST**
**Burt Lancaster**
Sgt. Milton Warden
**Montgomery Clift**
Robert E. Lee Prewitt
**Deborah Kerr**
Karen Holmes
**Donna Reed**
Lorene
**Frank Sinatra**
Angelo Maggio
**Philip Ober**
Capt. Dana Holmes
**Mickey Shaughnessy**
Sgt. Leva
**Harry Bellaver**
Mazzioli
**Ernest Borgnine**
Sgt. 'Fatso' Judson
**Jack Warden**
Corp. Buckley

**John Dennis**
Sgt. Ike Galovitch
**Merle Travis**
Sal Anderson
**Tim Ryan**
Sgt. Pete Karelsen
**Arthur Keegan**
Treadwell
**Barbara Morrison**
Mrs. Kipfer
[uncredited]
**Claude Akins**
Sgt. Baldy Dhom
**Robert Karnes**
Sgt. Turp Thornhill
**Robert Wilke**
Sgt. Henderson
**Douglas Henderson**
Corp. Champ Wilson
**Don Dubbins**
Friday Clark
**John L. Cason**
Corp. Paluso
**George Reeves**
Sgt. Maylon Stark
**Jean Willes**
Annette
**Delia Salvi**
Billie
**Angela Stevens**
Jean
**Mary Carver**
Nancy
**Vicki Bakken**
Suzanne
**Margaret Barstow**
Roxanne
**William Lundmark**
Bill
**Joan Shawlee**
Sandra

**Moana Gleason**
Rose
**Weaver Levy**
Bartender
**Brick Sullivan**
Military Guard
**Kristine Miller**
Georgette
**Al Sargent**
Nair
**Robert Pike**
Maj. Bonds
**Freeman Lusk**
Col. Wood
**Tyler McVey**
Maj. Stern
**Fay Roope**
Gen. Slater
**Carleton Young**
Col. Ayres
**Willis Bouchey**
Lt. Colonel
**John Bryant**
Capt. Ross

US Copyright Date
29 July 1953
US Releases
5 August 1953 (New York)
30 September 1953 (Los
Angeles)
US Distributor
Columbia Pictures

UK Release
13 November 1953
UK Distributor
Columbia Pictures
MPAA Certificate
Approval
No. 16582
13 reels
118 minutes

# Bibliography

### Archival/Unpublished Sources

Clift, Montgomery. Papers. New York Library for the Performing Arts. New York, NY.

Department of Defense Files. RG 330, box 705. National Archives, College Park, MD.

Jones, James. Papers. Beinecke Rare Book and Manuscript Library. Yale University. New Haven, CT.

'An Oral History with Daniel Taradash'. Interviewed by Barbara Hall (Beverly Hills, CA: Academy of Motion Picture Arts and Sciences, Oral History Program, 2001), 664 pp.

Taradash, Daniel. Papers. Western Heritage Center. Cheyenne, WY.

Zinnemann, Fred. Papers. AMPAS. Beverly Hills, CA.

### Books and Articles

'A New Role for Deborah Kerr', *Woman's Own* (12 November 1953).

Bailey, Beth and David Farber, *The First Strange Place: Race and Sex in World War II Hawaii* (Baltimore, MD: Johns Hopkins University Press, 1992).

Bell-Metereau, Rebecca, '1953: Movies and Our Secret Lives', in Murray Pomerance (ed.), *American Cinema in the 1950s: Themes and Variations* (New Brunswick, NJ: Rutgers University Press, 2005), pp. 89–110.

Bérubé, Allan, *Coming Out under Fire: The History of Gay Men and Women in World War II* (New York: Penguin, 1990).

Biskind, Peter, *Seeing Is Believing: How I Learned to Stop Worrying and Love the Fifties* (London: Pluto Press, 1983).

Bosworth, Patricia, *Montgomery Clift: A Biography* (New York: Limelight, 1978).

Boyle, Hal, 'Writer No Longer Low Man of Films, Says Taradash', *Mirror-News* (7 January 1959).

Buford, Kate, *Lancaster: An American Life* (New York: Knopf, 2000).

'Censored', *Look* (25 August 1953).

Clark, Suzanne, *Cold Warriors: Manliness on Trial in the Rhetoric of the West* (Carbondale: Southern Illinois University Press, 2000).

Daugherty, Frank, 'Buddy Adler, Exhibitor-Producer', *New York Times* (16 April 1950).

Denton, Charles, 'A Good Girl Makes Good', *Los Angeles Examiner, TV Weekly* (12 March 1961).

Douglas, Susan, *Where the Girls Are: Growing Up Female with the Media* (New York: Times Books, 1995).

Farber, Manny, '*From Here to Eternity*', *Nation* (29 August 1953).

Flood, Alison, 'Censored Gay Sex Scenes in *From Here to Eternity* Revealed', *Guardian* (13 November 2009).

Freedland, Michael, *All the Way: A Biography of Frank Sinatra* (London: Weidenfeld & Nicolson, 1997).

'*From Here to Eternity*', *Colliers* (7 August 1953).

—, *Hollywood Reporter* (29 July 1953).

—, *Motion Picture Daily* (29 July 1953).

—, *Variety* (29 July 1953).

Hendler, Jane, *Best-Sellers and Their Film Adaptations in Postwar America* (New York: Peter Lang, 2001).

'Inside Buddy Adler', *Screen Producers Guild Journal* vol. 2 no. 12 (1954), pp. 2–4.

Itria, Helen, 'Burt Lancaster: The Story of a Hard Man', *Look* vol 17 no. 21 (October 1953), pp. 94–5.

Jones, James, *From Here to Eternity* (New York: Scribners, 1951).

Leff, Leonard and Simmons, Jerold, *The Dame in the Kimono* (London: Weidenfeld & Nicolson, 1990).

'The Love Scene You'll Talk About', *Picturegoer* (14 November 1953).

McClay, Howard, 'Buddy Adler', *Los Angeles Daily News* (2 October 1952).

Miller, Gabriel (ed.), *Fred Zinnemann Interviews* (Jackson: University Press of Mississippi, 2005).

Morgenstern, Joe, 'Worldly Wisdom', *Wall Street Journal* (13 May 2006).

National Centre for Health Statistics, *Marriage and Divorce Statistics United States, 1867–1967*, series 21 number 24 (December 1973).

Rosenberg, Emily, *A Date Which Will Live: Pearl Harbor in American Memory* (Durham, NC: Duke University Press, 2003).

Sandoz, Mari, *Cheyenne Autumn* (New York: McGraw-Hill Book Company, Inc., 1953).

Schallert, Edwin, '*From Here to Eternity* Blasts Viewers with Atomic Power', *Los Angeles Times* (1 October 1953).

Schmidt, M. A., 'On the Elevation of Mr. Adler', *New York Times* (27 September 1953).

Scott, A. O., 'War Is Hell, But Very Pretty', *New York Times* (25 May 2001).

Smyth, J. E., *Fred Zinnemann and the Cinema of Resistance* (Jackson: University Press of Mississippi, 2014).

—, 'James Jones, Columbia Pictures, and the Historical Confrontations of *From Here to Eternity*', in Peter Rollins and John E. O'Connor (eds), *Why We Fought: America's Wars in Film and Television* (Lexington: University Press of Kentucky, 2008), pp. 283–302.

Thomas, Bob, 'Adler Passing Mourned by All in Film Business', *Mirror-News* (3 September 1960).

—, *King Cohn: The Life and Times of Hollywood Mogul Harry Cohn* [1967] (Beverly Hills, CA: New Millennium Press, 2000).

Turan, Kenneth, '*Eternity* Is, Quite Simply, Timeless', *Los Angeles Times* (5 December 2003).

Turner, Frederick Jackson, *The Frontier in American History* (New York: Henry Holt & Co., 1921).

Whitfield, Stephen J., *The Culture of the Cold War* [1991] (Baltimore, MD: Johns Hopkins University Press, 1996).

Winsten, Archer, 'Reviewing Stand', *New York Post* (2 August 1953).

—, '*From Here to Eternity* Bows at Capitol with Huge Cast, Five Starring Roles', *New York Times* (6 August 1953).

Zinnemann, Fred, *An Autobiography* (London: Scribners, 1992).

Zunser, Jesse, '*From Here to Eternity*', *Cue*, (8 August 1953), p. 16.